DECADENT
DESSERTS

In all Rodale cookbooks, our mission is to provide delicious and nutritious recipes. Our recipes also meet the standards of the Rodale Test Kitchen for dependability, ease, practicality, and, most of all, great taste. To give us your comments, call (800) 848-4735.

RODALE'S
New
Classics™

DECADENT
DESSERTS

By Anne Egan

RODALE

Rodale's New Classics and Favorite Recipes Made Easy for Today's Lifestyle are trademarks of Rodale Inc.

Printed in China.

Cover and Interior Designer: Richard Kershner
Front Cover Recipe: Chocolate Cheesecake (page 38)

Library of Congress Cataloging-in-Publication Data

Egan, Anne.

   Decadent desserts / By Anne Egan.

       p. cm. — (Rodale's new classics)

Includes index.

   ISBN 1–57954–448–7

   1. Desserts   I. Title.

   TX773 .E335   2001

   641.6—dc21   2001000586

Distributed to the book trade by St. Martin's Press

2 4 6 8 10 9 7 5 3 1 paperback

Visit us on the Web at www.rodalestore.com, or call us toll-free at (800) 848-4735.

RODALE

WE **INSPIRE** AND **ENABLE** PEOPLE TO IMPROVE
THEIR LIVES AND THE WORLD AROUND THEM

TROPICAL FRUIT CAKE
Page 22

SIMPLE CHOCOLATE PUDDING
Page 76

Contents

CHERRY PIE
Page 45

CHOCOLATE CANNOLI
Page 106

Introduction

Decadent desserts—sounds like something that one orders in a restaurant, leaving these tricky delights to the pastry chef to perfect. But even novice cooks can prepare these impressive, delicious delights with minimal work. Some of these homemade treats are made simpler by using prepared products such as instant pudding mix or packaged crepes. Others start from scratch using my classic pie crust or a simple pastry cream. Either way, the results are spectacular. The secret to creating great-tasting desserts every time is to use the best-quality ingredients available. Since a decadent dessert is more a treat than a nightly ritual, these recipes call for heavy cream, butter, puff pastry, and all the features of the best confections. So don't worry that you're not using low-fat products; after all, we all need some fat in our diets, and what better way to get it than from desserts! Relax and enjoy a bit of decadence; I am sure you and your family deserve it.

Rodale's New Classics is about keeping your life simple while enjoying the process of baking and cooking. Preparing delicious homemade desserts is a process I find relaxing and rewarding. Most of these recipes require minimal work but provide maximum results. Follow these simple basics for success every time.

Cakes

From a classic birthday cake to a simple pound cake, when baking cakes, you'll need to keep several basics in mind to ensure a perfect outcome every time.

Always preheat the oven. This way, you'll be certain that it's the correct temperature by the time you've combined all the ingredients. Otherwise, the cake won't bake properly, and you won't be able to rely on the baking time in the recipe.

Measure the ingredients accurately. Spoon flour and other dry ingredients into the exact size measuring cup needed; then level off any excess with a table knife. Measure oil, milk, and similar ingredients in a liquid measuring cup, and place the cup on a flat surface to check the amount. To easily measure butter, buy sticks that show tablespoon measurements right on the wrapper, then cut the amount you need.

Prepare cake pans properly. Cakes are almost always baked in a greased pan. Use butter, shortening, or cooking spray to grease. Delicate cakes often call for the pan to be greased and floured. This assures the cake will remove from the pan evenly. Use waxed or parchment paper when a recipe calls for paper-lined pans.

Use the right rack. Unless otherwise specified, bake cakes and all other baked goods on the center rack of your oven.

Adjust for altitude. If you live above an altitude of 3,000 feet, increase the oven temperature by 25°F and decrease the baking time slightly.

Check for doneness. Test cakes with a wooden pick 5 to 10 minutes before they're supposed to be done. This allows a margin for error since each oven bakes slightly differently. In most recipes, a clean pick means that the cake is done. Always set the cake in the pan on a rack to cool. Follow directions whether to cool completely in the pan or remove from the pan after 10 minutes to the rack to cool. Cakes left in the pan for too long will stick to the pan and create a mess upon removal.

The finishing touch. Cakes can be frosted, iced, or dusted with confectioners' sugar or cocoa. Don't always feel locked in to the method suggested in the recipes. Most cakes are versatile, so if you are in a hurry, forgo the frosting and dust with sugar or a simple glaze made by combining confectioners' sugar with a liquid, such as citrus juice, milk, or melted chocolate.

Pies and Tarts

Pies and tarts both use crusts to cradle a variety of delicious fillings, including all manner of fruit as well as chocolate, fluffy whipped cream concoctions—you name it. In this book, I've incorporated the same basic dough into many of the pie and tart recipes with sensational results. If you are pressed for time, feel free to substitute a prepared crust for the homemade one. Here are some tips for mastering crusts.

Mixing the dough. Homemade pie and tart crusts are steps above the prepared ones, mostly because of the addition of rich butter to the crust. Simply combine the flour, salt, and sugar (if called for) and then cut in the butter and shortening with a pastry blender or two knives used scissor fashion. The key is to work the dough until it resembles small, coarse crumbs. Add the ice water, a few tablespoons at a time. Be sure not to overwork the dough, but do work the water in until it is very well combined. Form the dough into a disk, wrap in plastic wrap, and place in the refrigerator until ready to roll. Doughs made with all shortening don't need this step, while those with butter are best when chilled slightly. I use half

butter and half shortening to create a rich, flaky crust.

Roll it right. Since the dough needs to extend up the sides and edge of pie plates, roll the dough out to 2" larger than the pie plate. Press into the bottom and sides of the pan, letting any extra hang over the edges. Cut the crust so that it extends evenly over the rim, then roll it underneath the dough and crimp to form a decorative crust.

Prebaking crusts. Some recipes don't require baking until after the filling is added to the crust, but others call for baking the crust before filling it. When baking a crust without the filling in it, pierce the dough a few times with a fork to prevent it from bubbling.

Watch for browning. Once your crust is filled and in the oven, watch it carefully to make sure that it doesn't brown too quickly. If it does, cover the crust with foil during the last 10 to 20 minutes of baking.

Make it pretty. To make a pie with a "lid," make enough dough for two pie crusts and use the second crust to cover the filling. If you like, you can cut slits in the top for an old-fashioned look. Or, use the second batch of dough to make a lattice top by cutting the dough into strips and criss-crossing them on top of the pie. You can even make cutout shapes and arrange them in a decorative fashion.

To give the top of your pies and tarts a lovely glaze, simply brush with beaten egg yolk.

Make it different. Many pies use crumb crusts instead of pastry crusts. These are made with a simple mixture of crushed cookies, sugar, and butter. These are especially fun to use because you can easily change the flavor of the crust simply by changing the crumbs. Some favorites include crumbs made from cinnamon graham crackers, gingersnaps, chocolate cookies, and vanilla wafers.

Puddings, Custards, and Fools

This category includes a large assortment of desserts that all have a creamy element. Some are simpler or fancier than others, but all deliver a thick, smooth texture and deeply rich flavor. Mastering them is easy—here's how.

Perfecting the consistency. Puddings and custards are often cooked in a saucepan on the stove top. Eggs add a rich creaminess to the mixture but must be handled with care. To begin, cook the liquid, cornstarch, and flavorings until they thicken. Then, whisk about 1 cup of this mixture into beaten eggs to heat them, beginning their cooking process and preventing curdling. This step is known as tempering the eggs. Whisk the egg mixture back into the pudding, which cooks just until thickened.

Beat it. Two key components of these desserts are whipped cream and beaten egg whites, often in the same recipe. Always work with a clean, dry bowl and beaters. Keep cream cold until beating. You may even wish to chill the bowl and beaters for a few minutes before starting. This will produce the greatest volume. Once the cream reaches the soft peak stage, watch it carefully, as it won't take long to get to stiff peaks. Egg whites reach their greatest volume when at room temperature, so place the whites on the counter for a few minutes before beating. Because whites will not beat up with any fat present, always beat them first if a recipe calls for both beaten whites and cream. After beating the whites, there is no need to clean the beaters; the cream will beat up with some of the whites in the mixture.

Bake it right. Baked custards such as flans and crème brûlée are baked in custard cups in a pan of water called a water bath. This ensures that the custards bake evenly without browning on the outer edges.

Chill it. If you plan to chill your pudding before serving it, cover it with a piece of waxed paper or plastic wrap right on the surface. This will prevent a skin from forming.

Cannolis, Crepes, and Other Confections

When many of us think *decadent*, images of classic pastries and confections may often come to mind—the kind you imagine nibbling over coffee at an outdoor café.

Make it easy. These delights are a breeze to make thanks to the array of prepared products available. Prebaked cannoli shells, crepes, and blintzes are available in supermarkets, bakeries, and some delis.

Whether a creamy, simple pudding or a rich apple strudel, I hope you will have fun impressing your family and friends with these luscious desserts. Enjoy!

BLUE-RIBBON CAKES

Rich Chocolate Layer Cake

Cake

1½ cups unbleached all-purpose flour

½ cup unsweetened cocoa powder

1 tablespoon instant espresso powder

1 teaspoon baking soda

½ cup butter, softened

1 cup sugar

1 egg

1 teaspoon vanilla extract

½ cup buttermilk

½ cup hot water

Frosting

1½ cups sugar

3 egg whites

¼ cup water

1 teaspoon cream of tartar

1 teaspoon vanilla extract

¼ cup unsweetened cocoa powder

Classic layer cake is always a crowd pleaser, especially when crowned with fluffy chocolate frosting. For those who can never get enough chocolate, try decorating the top with pretty chocolate curls.

To make the cake: Preheat the oven to 350°F. Grease two 8" round cake pans.

In a medium bowl, combine the flour, cocoa powder, espresso powder, and baking soda.

In a large bowl, with an electric mixer on medium speed, beat the butter and sugar for 3 minutes, or until creamy. Add the egg and vanilla extract. Beat on low speed until creamy.

With the mixer on low speed, gradually add the flour mixture, alternating with the buttermilk and water. Pour the batter into the prepared cake pans. Bake for 25 minutes, or until a wooden pick inserted in the center comes out clean.

Cool on a rack for 10 minutes. Remove from the pan and place on the rack to cool completely.

To make the frosting: Meanwhile, in the top of a double boiler, combine the sugar, egg whites, water, and cream of tartar. Place over a saucepan of simmering water. With clean beaters and the mixer on high speed, beat for 5 minutes, or until soft peaks form. Add the vanilla extract and beat for 4 minutes, or until the mixture is thick and glossy and registers 160°F on an instant-read thermometer. Remove from the heat. Sift the cocoa over the frosting and gently fold in. Allow to cool completely, about 20 minutes.

Place 1 cooled cake layer on a serving plate. Evenly spread the top with frosting. Top with the remaining cake layer and spread the top with frosting. Spread the remaining frosting over the sides.

Makes 12 servings

Per serving: 316 calories, 5 g protein, 56 g carbohydrates, 9 g fat, 40 mg cholesterol, 2 g fiber, 219 mg sodium

Chocolate Cherry Cake

Topping

1   **can (15 ounces) cherry pie and cake filling**

½   **tablespoon Grand Marnier**

Cake

2   **cups cake flour (see tip on page 27)**

2   **teaspoons baking powder**

½   **teaspoon baking soda**

¼   **teaspoon salt**

½   **cup unsweetened cocoa powder**

½   **ounce semisweet chocolate, finely grated**

1   **teaspoon instant espresso powder**

1   **cup packed brown sugar**

⅓   **cup unsweetened applesauce**

¼   **cup canola oil**

2   **eggs**

1   **cup milk**

2   **teaspoons vanilla extract**

⅓   **cup cherry all-fruit spread**

½   **cup heavy or whipping cream**

     Semisweet chocolate curls (optional)

This cake is so beautiful, everyone will think you stopped off at a bakery on the way home!

To make the topping: In a small bowl, combine the cherry filling and Grand Marnier. Set aside.

To make the cake: Preheat the oven to 350°F. Grease two 8" round cake pans.

In a large bowl, combine the flour, baking powder, baking soda, salt, cocoa powder, chocolate, espresso powder, and brown sugar.

In a medium bowl, combine the applesauce, oil, eggs, milk, and vanilla extract. Stir the applesauce mixture into the flour mixture and mix until the batter is smooth.

Spread the batter in the prepared cake pans. Bake for 20 minutes, or until a wooden pick inserted in the center comes out clean. Cool on a rack for 10 minutes. Remove from the pan and place on the rack to cool completely.

Place 1 cooled cake layer on a serving plate. Evenly cover with the all-fruit spread. Top with the remaining cake layer. Evenly spoon the cherry topping over the top, leaving a 1" border around the rim.

In a small bowl, with clean beaters and the mixer on medium-high speed, beat the heavy cream until soft peaks form. Decorate the rim of the cake with the whipped cream and spread on the sides of the cake. Garnish with the chocolate curls, if using.

Makes 12 servings

Per serving: 320 calories, 4 g protein, 53 g carbohydrates, 11 g fat, 52 mg cholesterol, 2 g fiber, 210 mg sodium

Silken Glazed Chocolate Espresso Cake

Cake

¾   **cup butter**

6   **ounces bittersweet chocolate, chopped**

2   **teaspoons instant espresso powder**

1   **teaspoon vanilla extract**

¼   **teaspoon ground cinnamon**

4   **eggs, separated**

⅛   **teaspoon salt**

¾   **cup sugar**

⅓   **cup unbleached all-purpose flour**

Glaze

⅓   **cup heavy cream or whipping cream**

2½ **ounces bittersweet chocolate, finely chopped**

Coffee lovers will savor the richness and dreamy flavor of this melt-in-your-mouth espresso cake. The glaze will send you into chocolate heaven.

To make the cake: Preheat the oven to 350°F. Grease an 8" round cake pan, then line with waxed paper or parchment paper.

In a small saucepan over low heat, melt the butter and chocolate, stirring occasionally. Remove from the heat and stir in the espresso powder, vanilla extract, and cinnamon. Set aside to cool slightly.

In a medium bowl, with an electric mixer on high speed, beat the egg whites and salt until stiff peaks form. Set aside.

In a large bowl, with the mixer on medium speed, using the same beaters, beat the egg yolks and sugar for 2 minutes, or until ribbony. While beating, gradually add in the chocolate mixture, then the flour, until blended. Using a rubber spatula, fold in the egg whites just until blended. Pour the batter into the prepared cake pan.

Bake for 30 minutes, or until set (a wooden pick inserted in the center will not come out clean).

Run a knife around the rim of the cake to loosen it from the sides. Cool on a rack for 15 minutes. Remove the cake from the pan and place on the rack to cool completely.

To make the glaze: In a small saucepan over medium heat, bring the cream to a boil; remove from the heat. Add the chocolate and let stand for 5 minutes. Whisk until smooth and let cool slightly. Pour the glaze over the cake.

Makes 12 servings
Per serving: 315 calories, 4 g protein, 27 g carbohydrates, 23 g fat, 113 mg cholesterol, 2 g fiber, 180 mg sodium

German Chocolate Cake

Cake

2   cups unbleached all-purpose flour

½   cup sugar

⅓   cup unsweetened cocoa powder

1   tablespoon baking powder

1   teaspoon cinnamon

¼   teaspoon salt

½   cup butter

1   cup light cream

Topping

1½ cups caramel topping

1½ cups pecan halves, toasted and broken into large pieces

1   cup flaked coconut

The hallmark of German chocolate cake is the buttery coconut-pecan frosting. This chocolate and cinnamon cake goes nicely with steaming cups of cappuccino.

To make the cake: Preheat the oven to 350°F. Grease two 8" round cake pans.

In a large bowl, combine the flour, sugar, cocoa, baking powder, cinnamon, and salt.

With a pastry blender or fork, cut the butter into the flour mixture until it resembles coarse crumbs. Stir in the cream, mixing just until blended. Evenly divide the batter into the prepared pans.

Bake for 18 minutes, or until a wooden pick inserted in the center comes out clean. Cool on a rack for 10 minutes. Remove from the pans and place on the rack to cool completely.

To make the topping: In a medium saucepan, heat the caramel topping for 3 minutes, or until hot. Remove from the heat and stir in the pecans and coconut.

Pierce the tops of the cake layers with a fork in several places. Place 1 cooled cake layer on a serving plate. Spread half of the topping over the layer. Top with the remaining layer and topping.

Makes 12 servings

Per serving: 448 calories, 6 g protein, 57 g carbohydrates, 25 g fat, 36 mg cholesterol, 3 g fiber, 384 mg sodium

COOKING TIP

To freeze, wrap the cooled cake in freezer-quality plastic wrap, then in freezer-quality foil. To use, thaw overnight in the refrigerator.

Chocolate Angel Food Cake

1 cup unbleached all-purpose flour

1 cup sugar

⅓ cup unsweetened cocoa powder

½ teaspoon ground cinnamon

10 egg whites, at room temperature

1¼ teaspoons cream of tartar

1½ teaspoons vanilla extract

2 cups assorted fresh berries

Confectioners' sugar

Angel food cake rises to new heights with this chocolate-rich recipe. For an added treat, drizzle with melted chocolate or caramel sauce.

Preheat the oven to 350°F.

Sift the flour, ½ cup of the sugar, cocoa, and cinnamon into a medium bowl.

Place the egg whites in a large bowl. With an electric mixer on medium speed, beat until foamy. Add the cream of tartar and beat until soft peaks form. Gradually beat in the remaining ½ cup sugar and vanilla extract. Continue beating until stiff peaks form.

Fold in the flour mixture 1 cup at a time, just until blended

Place in a 10" tube pan, spreading evenly and deflating any large air pockets with a knife.

Bake for 40 minutes, or until a wooden pick inserted in the center comes out clean. Cool upside down on a bottle neck for 40 minutes. Turn right side up and run a knife around the rim of the cake to loosen it from the sides. Remove the cake from the pan and place on a rack to cool completely.

To serve, top the cake with the berries and sprinkle with confectioners' sugar.

Makes 12 servings

Per serving: 134 calories, 5 g protein, 29 g carbohydrates, 1 g fat, 0 mg cholesterol, 2 g fiber, 47 mg sodium

Grandma's Best Gingerbread

2   **cups unbleached all-purpose flour**
1   **teaspoon ground cinnamon**
1   **teaspoon baking soda**
1   **teaspoon ginger**
½   **teaspoon salt**
1   **cup boiling water**
½   **cup molasses**
1   **cup sugar**
½   **cup butter**
1   **egg**

Everybody's favorite when warm from the oven, this spicy gingerbread is moist yet light. The perfect combination of ginger and molasses earns this recipe a "Grandma's best" rating.

Preheat the oven to 350°F. Grease a 9" x 9" baking pan.

In a medium bowl, combine the flour, cinnamon, baking soda, ginger, and salt.

In a glass measuring cup, stir together the water and molasses.

In a medium bowl, with an electric mixer on medium speed, beat the sugar and butter for 3 minutes, or until light and fluffy. With the mixer on low speed, add the egg and beat for 1 minute. Alternately add the flour mixture and molasses mixture, beating until just combined.

Pour into the prepared baking pan and bake for 45 minutes, or until a wooden pick inserted in the center comes out clean. Cool on a rack 20 minutes and serve warm, or cool completely.

Makes 9 servings
Per serving: 343 calories, 4 g protein, 56 g carbohydrates, 12 g fat, 53 mg cholesterol, 0 g fiber, 394 mg sodium

COOKING TIP

Try serving gingerbread with fresh whipped cream. For more flavor, add a teaspoon of raspberry liqueur to the cream before whipping. Each cup of heavy cream yields 2 cups whipped.

Make hard sauce by beating together butter, sugar (confectioners' or brown will also work), and a flavoring (a liqueur or extract) until smooth. Refrigerate until hard, then spoon onto the gingerbread.

Boston Cream Pie

Cake

2   cups unbleached all-purpose flour

2   teaspoons baking powder

¼   teaspoon baking soda

½   teaspoon salt

1   cup sugar

½   cup butter, softened

2   eggs

4   ounces sour cream

½   cup milk

1   tablespoon vanilla extract

Filling

1   package (4-serving size) vanilla instant pudding and pie filling

1¼ cups half-and-half

1   tablespoon hazelnut or orange liqueur (optional)

Topping

¾   cup hot fudge or chocolate sauce

When is a pie not a pie? When it's a Boston cream pie! This longtime favorite boasts a custard filling sandwiched between two lovely layers of yellow cake. The chocolate topping is the perfect finishing touch.

To make the cake: Preheat the oven to 350°F. Grease two 9" round cake pans and dust with flour.

In a medium bowl, combine the flour, baking powder, baking soda, and salt.

In another large bowl, with an electric mixer on medium speed, beat together the sugar and butter for 4 minutes, or until creamy. Add the eggs, sour cream, milk, and vanilla extract. Beat for 1 minute on low speed, scraping the bowl often. Beat on high speed for 2 minutes, or until smooth.

With the mixer on low speed, gradually add the flour mixture and beat until the batter is light and fluffy.

Evenly divide the batter between the prepared pans. Bake for 35 minutes, or until a wooden pick inserted in the center comes out clean.

Cool on a rack for 10 minutes. Remove from the pan and place on the rack to cool completely.

To make the filling: In a medium bowl, stir together the pudding mix, half-and-half, and liqueur (if using) until blended. Cover with plastic wrap flush to the surface and refrigerate for 30 minutes.

To assemble: Place 1 cooled cake layer on a serving plate. Spread the pudding mixture over the cake. Top with the remaining cake layer. Pour the topping in the center of the top layer and gently spread so that it drips over the edges.

Makes 16 servings

Per serving: 311 calories, 5 g protein, 45 g carbohydrates, 13 g fat, 55 mg cholesterol, 0 g fiber, 475 mg sodium

Tropical Fruit Cake

1 **package (18 ounces) yellow cake mix**

1 **can (20 ounces) unsweetened crushed pineapple**

8 **ounces cream cheese**

2 **cups milk**

1 **package (4-serving size) instant vanilla-flavored pudding and pie filling**

2 **tablespoons rum or ½ teaspoon rum extract**

1 **cup whipped topping**

1 **can (15½ ounces) mandarin oranges, drained**

What a wonderful way to turn a box of cake mix into a sunny-tasting pineapple treat! It's the perfect dessert for potlucks.

Preheat the oven to 325°F or according to cake mix package directions. Grease a 13" x 9" baking dish.

Prepare the cake mix according to package directions. Pour into the prepared baking dish. Bake according to package directions.

Cool in the pan on a rack. Poke holes all over the cake with the handle of a small wooden spoon. Pour the pineapple (with juice) over the cake.

In a large bowl, with an electric mixer on medium speed, beat the cream cheese until smooth. Add the milk, pudding mix, and rum or rum extract. Beat for 3 minutes. Pour over the pineapple. Top with the whipped topping and then the oranges. Cover and refrigerate for at least 4 hours.

Makes 12 servings
Per serving: 348 calories, 5 g protein, 49 g carbohydrates, 14 g fat, 27 mg cholesterol, 1 g fiber, 377 mg sodium

Simple Cardamom-Orange Cake

- 1¾ cups unbleached all-purpose flour
- 2 teaspoons ground cardamom
- 1½ teaspoons baking powder
- ¾ cup sugar
- ½ cup butter
- 2 eggs
- ¼ cup orange juice
- 1 tablespoon grated orange peel
- 1 teaspoon vanilla extract
- ½ cup milk

Here's an easy coffee cake you can whip up in a jiffy. The cake will keep for 2 to 3 days at room temperature if well-wrapped.

Preheat the oven to 350°F. Grease an 8" round baking pan.

In a medium bowl, combine the flour, cardamom, and baking powder.

In a large bowl, with an electric mixer on medium speed, beat the sugar and butter for 4 minutes, or until creamy. Add the eggs and beat until blended. Add the orange juice, orange peel, and vanilla extract and beat until blended. With the mixer on low speed, gradually add the flour mixture, alternating with the milk. Place the batter into the prepared baking pan.

Bake for 30 minutes, or until a wooden pick inserted in the center comes out clean. Cool on a rack for 10 minutes. Remove from the pan and place on the rack to cool completely.

Makes 12 servings

Per serving: 212 calories, 4 g protein, 28 g carbohydrates, 10 g fat, 59 mg cholesterol, 0 g fiber, 148 mg sodium

Coconut Cream Bundt Cake

2 cups sifted cake flour (see tip on page 27)

2 teaspoons baking powder

½ teaspoon baking soda

½ teaspoon salt

4 egg whites

½ teaspoon cream of tartar

4 egg yolks

1 cup sugar

1¼ cups cream of coconut

2 teaspoons vanilla extract

⅔ cup flaked coconut

The creamy sweetness of coconut really shines through in this Bundt cake, giving it a rich, satisfying taste. It's quite pretty as is, but for special occasions, you could try drizzling it lightly with your favorite glaze.

Preheat the oven to 350°F. Grease a 10" Bundt or tube pan.

In a medium bowl, combine the flour, baking powder, baking soda, and salt.

In a large bowl, with an electric mixer on medium speed, beat the egg whites until frothy. Add the cream of tartar and beat until stiff peaks form.

In another medium bowl, with the mixer on medium speed, beat the egg yolks, sugar, cream of coconut, and vanilla extract for 3 minutes, or until blended. With the mixer on low speed, gradually add the flour mixture. Fold in the egg whites and coconut.

Place the batter in the prepared cake pan. Bake for 35 minutes, or until a wooden pick inserted in the center comes out clean. Cool on a rack for 10 minutes. Remove from the pan and place on the rack to cool completely.

Makes 12 servings
Per serving: 253 calories, 5 g protein, 33 g carbohydrates, 12 g fat, 71 mg cholesterol, 1 g fiber, 239 mg sodium

Traditional Pound Cake

2¼ cups cake flour (see tip)
1 teaspoon baking powder
¼ teaspoon salt
1 cup butter, at room temperature
1 cup sugar
3 eggs
1 teaspoon grated lemon peel
1 teaspoon vanilla extract
½ cup (4 ounces) sour cream

Undoubtedly one of the most versatile cakes there is, pound cake fits the bill in oh-so-many ways. Serve as a dessert or for afternoon tea; try it plain or top with ice cream or fresh fruit; wrap it in decorative foil or plastic for a thoughtful homemade gift; or make several for a local bake sale—they'll sell like hotcakes!

Preheat the oven to 350°F. Grease a 9" x 5" loaf pan and dust lightly with flour.

In a medium bowl, combine the flour, baking powder, and salt. In a large bowl, with an electric mixer on medium speed, beat the butter and sugar for 4 minutes, or until creamy. Add the eggs, one at a time, beating well after each addition. Add the lemon peel and vanilla extract and beat until blended. With the mixer on low speed, gradually add the flour mixture, alternating with the sour cream.

Place the batter into the prepared pan. Bake for 55 minutes, or until a wooden pick inserted in the center comes out clean. Cool on a rack for 10 minutes. Remove from the pan and place on the rack to cool completely.

Makes 16 servings
Per serving: 237 calories, 3 g protein, 24 g carbohydrates, 14 g fat, 75 mg cholesterol, 0 g fiber, 201 mg sodium

---

COOKING TIP

If you don't have cake flour, you can use unbleached all-purpose flour instead. For each cup of cake flour, substitute 1 cup minus 2 tablespoons unbleached all-purpose flour.

Apple-Raisin Crumb Cake

Streusel

¾ cup unbleached all-purpose flour

⅔ cup packed brown sugar

1 teaspoon ground cinnamon

3 tablespoons butter, cut into small pieces

Cake

2¼ cups unbleached all-purpose flour

1 teaspoon baking powder

1 teaspoon baking soda

½ teaspoon salt

¼ cup butter, softened

1 cup sugar

2 eggs

1 teaspoon vanilla extract

8 ounces sour cream

1 medium apple, peeled, cored, and finely chopped

⅓ cup golden raisins

This delicious crumbly cake is perfect for breakfast or for dessert. For a special autumn treat, serve it with cozy mugs of hot apple cider garnished with cinnamon sticks.

To make the streusel: In a small bowl, combine the flour, brown sugar, and cinnamon. Add the butter and work with your fingers or a fork to form crumbs.

To make the cake: Preheat the oven to 350°F. Grease a 9" x 9" cake pan.

In a medium bowl, combine the flour, baking powder, baking soda, and salt.

In another medium bowl, with an electric mixer on medium speed, beat the butter and sugar for 4 minutes, or until creamy. Add the eggs and vanilla extract, beating just until smooth. Alternately add the flour mixture and the sour cream, beating on low speed just until blended. Stir in the apple and raisins.

Place the batter into the prepared pan. Top with the streusel.

Bake for 40 minutes, or until a wooden pick inserted in the center comes out clean. Cool on a rack for 20 minutes and serve warm, or cool completely.

Makes 12 servings

Per serving: 366 calories, 6 g protein, 59 g carbohydrates, 12 g fat, 63 mg cholesterol, 1 g fiber, 333 mg sodium

Carrot-Apple Walnut Cake

Cake

1¼ cups unbleached all-purpose flour

1½ teaspoons baking powder

½ teaspoon baking soda

1 teaspoon ground cinnamon

¼ teaspoon freshly ground nutmeg

⅛ teaspoon salt

1 cup packed brown sugar

2 eggs

¼ cup vegetable oil

¼ cup applesauce

1½ cups grated carrots (about 2½ medium)

¼ cup raisins

¼ cup chopped walnuts

Frosting

4 ounces cream cheese

2 tablespoons butter

1 cup confectioners' sugar

½ teaspoon vanilla extract

¼ cup chopped walnuts

There's no better cake beneath luscious cream cheese frosting than good old-fashioned carrot cake. Add juicy, sweet raisins and a topping of crunchy walnuts, and voilá—a brand new classic!

To make the cake: Preheat the oven to 350°F. Grease an 8" x 8" baking pan.

In a medium bowl, combine the flour, baking powder, baking soda, cinnamon, nutmeg, and salt.

In a large bowl, with an electric mixer on medium speed, beat the brown sugar, eggs, oil, and applesauce until blended. Add the flour mixture and beat, stopping to scrape down the sides of the bowl once, until just combined. Stir in the carrots, raisins, and walnuts.

Place the batter into the prepared baking pan. Bake for 30 minutes, or until a wooden pick inserted in the center comes out clean. Cool completely in the pan on a rack.

To make the frosting: In a medium bowl, with an electric mixer on medium speed, beat the cream cheese, butter, confectioners' sugar, and vanilla extract until smooth. Spread evenly on top of the cooled cake.

Top with the walnuts.

Makes 9 servings

Per serving: 410 calories, 7 g protein, 57 g carbohydrates, 19 g fat, 68 mg cholesterol, 1 g fiber, 274 mg sodium

Orange Poppy Seed Cake

Cake

2	cups unbleached all-purpose flour
½	cup poppy seeds
½	teaspoon baking powder
½	teaspoon salt
4	egg whites
2	eggs
1¼	cups sugar
¼	cup canola oil
2	tablespoons grated orange peel
1	teaspoon vanilla extract
¾	cup orange juice

Glaze

¾	cup confectioners' sugar
1-2	tablespoons orange juice

The poppy seeds in this light cake lend a nutty taste, while the orange juice adds some zip. If you like, you can dust a little sifted confectioners' sugar over the glaze.

To make the cake: Preheat the oven to 350°F. Grease a 9" or 10" tube pan with a removable bottom and dust lightly with flour.

In a medium bowl, combine the flour, poppy seeds, baking powder, and salt.

In a large bowl, with an electric mixer on medium speed, beat the egg whites until soft peaks form.

In another bowl, using the same beater, beat the eggs and sugar until pale yellow and fluffy. Add the oil, orange peel, and vanilla extract, beating just until blended. Alternately add the flour mixture and the orange juice, beating on low speed just until blended.

Stir one-third of the egg whites into the batter, then fold in the rest. Place the batter into the prepared pan.

Bake for 40 minutes, or until a wooden pick inserted in the center comes out clean. The cake will rise and crack on top, then deflate a bit as it cools. Run a knife around the rim of the cake to loosen it from the sides. Cool on a rack for 15 minutes. Remove the cake from the pan and place on the rack to cool completely.

To make the glaze: In a small bowl, whisk together the confectioners' sugar and orange juice until smooth. Drizzle over the cooled cake.

Makes 12 servings

Per serving: 281 calories, 6 g protein, 47 g carbohydrates, 8 g fat, 35 mg cholesterol, 1 g fiber, 144 mg sodium

Cinnamon Swirl Cream Cheese Cake

Topping

⅔ cup unbleached all-purpose flour

¼ cup sugar

¼ teaspoon ground cinnamon

¼ cup butter

Cake

2½ cups unbleached all-purpose flour

1½ teaspoons baking powder

½ teaspoon salt

1½ cups sugar

1 cup butter

4 eggs

1 teaspoon vanilla extract

Filling

8 ounces cream cheese

½ cup sugar

1 egg

1 teaspoon vanilla extract

1 teaspoon ground cinnamon

Confectioners' sugar (optional)

Here's a Bundt cake with a cream cheese twist. A traditional crumb topping makes a fanciful appearance on the bottom of the cake for an added surprise.

Preheat the oven to 350°F. Grease a Bundt pan.

To make the topping: In a medium bowl, combine the flour, sugar, and cinnamon. Add the butter and work with your fingers or a fork to form crumbs.

To make the cake: In a medium bowl, combine the flour, baking powder, and salt; set aside.

In a large bowl, with an electric mixer on medium speed, beat the sugar and butter for 4 minutes, or until creamy. Beat in the eggs and vanilla extract until blended. Gradually add the flour mixture and beat on low speed just until blended.

To make the filling: In a medium bowl, with the mixer on medium speed, beat the cream cheese, sugar, egg, vanilla extract, and cinnamon for 4 minutes, or until creamy.

Spoon the cake batter into the prepared pan. Spoon the filling over the batter. Using a knife, gently marble the batter and filling. Sprinkle the crumb topping over the top, pressing gently into the batter. Bake for 50 minutes, or until the cake is set. Cool on a rack for 10 minutes. Remove from the pan and place on the rack to cool completely. Sprinkle with confectioners' sugar, if using.

Makes 16 servings

Per serving: 409 calories, 6 g protein, 48 g carbohydrates, 22 g fat, 123 mg cholesterol, 0 g fiber, 327 mg sodium

Strawberry Shortcakes

2   cups whole grain pastry flour

2   tablespoons packed brown sugar

2   teaspoons baking powder

¼   teaspoon baking soda

¼   cup butter, cut into small pieces

⅔   cup + 1 tablespoon buttermilk

1   tablespoon + ⅓ cup granulated sugar

2   pints strawberries, hulled and sliced

3   tablespoons orange juice

1   cup heavy cream

These dessert biscuits are jam-packed with sweet, juicy strawberries. If you like, you can vary the recipe by using other seasonal fresh fruits.

Preheat the oven to 400°F. Coat a baking sheet with cooking spray.

In a large bowl, combine the flour, brown sugar, baking powder, and baking soda. Using a pastry blender or 2 knives, cut in the butter until the mixture forms coarse crumbs. Add ⅔ cup of the buttermilk, stirring with a fork until the dough comes together.

Turn the dough out onto a lightly floured surface. Gently pat or roll to a ¾" thickness. Using a 3" round cutter or large glass, cut into 6 biscuits. (You may have to pat the dough scraps together to cut out all the biscuits.) Place on the prepared baking sheet. Brush with the remaining 1 tablespoon buttermilk. Sprinkle with 1 tablespoon of the granulated sugar.

Bake for 12 minutes, or until golden. Cool on a rack for 10 minutes. Remove from the pan and place on the rack to cool completely.

Meanwhile, in a large bowl, combine the strawberries, orange juice, and the remaining ⅓ cup granulated sugar. Let stand for 10 minutes, stirring occasionally.

In a medium bowl, with an electric mixer on medium-high speed, beat the heavy cream until soft peaks form.

Split the biscuits crosswise in half. On dessert plates, layer biscuits with berries in the center and on top. Top each with ⅓ cup of the whipped cream.

Makes 6 servings
Per serving: 466 calories, 8 g protein, 58 g carbohydrates, 24 g fat, 78 mg cholesterol, 6 g fiber, 317 mg sodium

New York Style Cheesecake

1½ cups graham cracker crumbs

¼ cup sugar

5 tablespoons butter, melted

4 packages (8 ounces each) cream cheese

1½ cups sugar

1 tablespoon grated lemon peel

1 teaspoon vanilla extract

¼ cup unbleached all-purpose flour

4 eggs

Fresh blueberries and strawberries for garnish

This cheesecake is so creamy and satisfying, you'll never bother with store-bought again. The graham cracker crust perfectly complements the smooth, lemony filling.

Preheat the oven to 350°F. Grease a 9" springform pan.

In a large bowl, combine the cracker crumbs, sugar, and butter. Press the mixture into the bottom and 1" up the sides of the prepared pan. Bake for 10 minutes, or until lightly browned. Cool on a rack.

In a large bowl, with an electric mixer on medium speed, beat the cream cheese, sugar, lemon peel, and vanilla extract for 4 minutes, or until creamy. Beat in the flour, then the eggs, until well-blended.

Pour the mixture into the prepared pan. Bake for 1 hour, or until set in the center. Remove from the oven and let cool on a rack to room temperature. Cover and refrigerate for at least 8 hours. Just before serving, top with fresh berries.

Makes 16 servings

Per serving: 373 calories, 7 g protein, 30 g carbohydrates, 26 g fat, 126 mg cholesterol, 0 g fiber, 270 mg sodium

Chocolate Cheesecake

1 box chocolate wafer cookies

4 tablespoons butter, melted

3 packages (8 ounces each) cream cheese, softened

1½ cups sugar

2 eggs

¾ cup cocoa powder

¼ teaspoon salt

1 tablespoon vanilla extract

½ teaspoon almond extract

½ cup heavy cream

Fresh raspberries for garnish

Mint sprigs for garnish

Dark. Dreamy. Delicious. All these words will come to mind with just one bite of this chocolate indulgence. A touch of almond extract adds the intensity that makes this a truly decadent dessert.

Preheat the oven to 325°F. Grease a 9" springform pan.

Place the cookies in a resealable plastic bag. Seal the bag and crush the cookies with a rolling pin to form coarse crumbs. Place in the prepared pan along with the butter. Stir to combine. Press the crumb mixture into the bottom and up the sides of the pan. Bake for 10 minutes, or until set. Cool on a rack.

Meanwhile, in a large bowl, with an electric mixer on medium speed, beat the cream cheese and sugar until smooth. Add the eggs, cocoa, salt, vanilla extract, and almond extract. Beat for 5 minutes, or until smooth and well-combined. Pour into the prepared crust. Bake for 1 hour and 15 minutes, or until the center is slightly soft. Turn off the oven and leave the cake in the oven for 1 hour. Remove to a rack and cool for 1 hour. Cover and refrigerate for 2 hours or overnight.

In a small bowl, with the mixer on medium-high speed, beat the heavy cream until soft peaks form. Decorate the cake with the whipped cream, raspberries, and mint.

Makes 16 servings

Per serving: 363 calories, 6 g protein, 34 g carbohydrates, 24 g fat, 93 mg cholesterol, 2 g fiber, 320 mg sodium

Ice Cream Jelly Roll

1 cup unbleached all-purpose flour
1 teaspoon baking powder
¼ teaspoon salt
4 eggs, separated
¾ cup sugar, divided
1 teaspoon vanilla extract
1 tablespoon confectioners' sugar
1 quart chocolate chip or other flavor ice cream, softened
⅔ cup hot fudge sauce, caramel sauce, or other topping

Here's a creative way to have your cake à la mode. Stretch your creative muscle even further by trying different ice cream-and-topping combos, like pistachio ice cream with strawberry sauce, or butter pecan with caramel sauce. The possibilities are nearly endless!

Preheat the oven to 375°F. Grease a 15" x 10" jelly-roll pan and dust with flour.

In a small bowl, combine the flour, baking powder, and salt.

In a medium bowl, with an electric mixer on medium speed, beat the egg whites until frothy. Slowly add ½ cup of the sugar and beat until stiff peaks form.

In a large bowl, with the mixer on high speed, using the same beaters, beat the egg yolks and the remaining ¼ cup sugar for 5 minutes, or until thick and lemon-colored. Add the vanilla extract. Add the flour mixture, alternately adding the egg white mixture, and fold just until blended.

Place the batter into the prepared pan and smooth it evenly. Bake for 8 minutes, or just until the top springs back when lightly touched in the center.

While the cake bakes, sprinkle a clean dish towel evenly with the confectioners' sugar.

Loosen the edges of the baked cake and immediately invert onto the towel. Starting from a short end, roll the cake, rolling the towel into the cake. Cool completely on a rack. Carefully unroll the cake and remove the towel. Spread the inside of the cake with the softened ice cream; reroll the cake. Wrap in plastic wrap or foil and freeze for at least 30 minutes. To serve, place the cake on a serving plate and drizzle with the hot fudge or caramel sauce.

Makes 12 servings
Per serving: 272 calories, 6 g protein, 40 g carbohydrates, 10 g fat, 95 mg cholesterol, 0 g fiber, 212 mg sodium

MEMORABLE
PIES AND TARTS

Blueberry Pie

2   recipes Basic Pie Crust (see tip)

1   cup sugar

⅓   cup unbleached all-purpose flour

½   teaspoon grated lemon peel

½   teaspoon cinnamon

4   cups fresh or thawed frozen blueberries

This easy pie is packed with a big blast of blueberries. A sprinkle of lemon and cinnamon adds some sassiness. Simple yet sensational!

Preheat the oven to 425°F.

Roll each piece of dough into an 11" circle. Place one crust in a 9" pie plate. Firmly press the dough against the bottom and sides of the pan.

In a large bowl, combine the sugar, flour, lemon peel, cinnamon, and blueberries. Place the filling into the prepared crust.

Place the second crust over the pie filling. Fold both edges of the dough under and crimp the crust. Using a sharp knife, make slits in the top. Bake for 10 minutes. Reduce the oven temperature to 350°F and bake for 25 minutes, or until golden brown and bubbly. To prevent overbrowning, cover the edge of the crust with foil if necessary during the last 15 to 20 minutes of baking. Cool on a rack for at least 2 hours.

Makes 10 servings

Per serving: 445 calories, 6 g protein, 61 g carbohydrates, 21 g fat, 26 g cholesterol, 2 g fiber, 122 g sodium

COOKING TIP

To make a 9" Basic Pie Crust, in a large bowl, combine 1½ cups unbleached all-purpose flour and ¼ teaspoon salt. Cut in ¼ cup unsalted butter and ¼ cup vegetable shortening until the mixture resembles coarse crumbs. Sprinkle 2 to 5 tablespoons ice water over the crumbs and toss with a fork until the dough holds together. Gather the mixture into a ball and press into a thick disk. Cover and refrigerate for 15 to 30 minutes before rolling out.

Cherry Pie

1 recipe Basic Pie Crust
   (see tip on page 42)

4 cups fresh or canned
   pitted tart cherries

1 cup sugar

3 tablespoons quick-
   cooking tapioca

½ teaspoon grated lemon
   peel

¼ teaspoon freshly ground
   nutmeg

This pretty pie uses some of the dough to decorate the top with lovely hearts—perfect for a romantic Valentine's Day dessert. If you like, try different shapes for other special occasions, perhaps bells for a bridal shower or stars for the Fourth of July.

Preheat the oven to 425°F.

Reserve ⅓ cup of the pie dough. Roll the remaining dough out to an 11" circle. Place the dough in a 9" round pie plate. Firmly press the dough against the bottom and sides of the pan. Fold the edges under and crimp the crust. Using a fork, pierce the bottom of the crust all over. Bake for 8 minutes, or until browned. Place on a rack.

Reduce the oven temperature to 375°F.

Roll the reserved dough out to ⅛" thickness. Using a cookie cutter or sharp knife, cut out decorative shapes, such as hearts or stars. Set aside.

Meanwhile, in a large saucepan, combine the cherries, sugar, tapioca, lemon peel, and nutmeg. Let the mixture stand for 5 minutes. Place over medium heat and cook, stirring, for 10 minutes, or until thickened.

Place the filling in the prepared pie crust. Place the cutouts over the filling. Bake for 25 minutes, or until the cutouts are golden brown and the juices begin to bubble. Cool on a rack for at least 2 hours.

Makes 10 servings

Per serving: 277 calories, 3 g protein, 44 g carbohydrates, 10 g fat, 13 mg cholesterol, 1 g fiber, 61 mg sodium

Homestyle Apple Pie

2   **recipes Basic Pie Crust (see tip on page 42)**

1   **lemon**

6   **medium Gala or other baking apples, peeled, cored, and cut into ½" slices (about 10 cups); see tip**

3   **tablespoons unbleached all-purpose flour**

¾   **cup + 1 teaspoon packed brown sugar**

1½ **teaspoons ground cinnamon**

1   **egg, beaten**

This down-home all-American favorite will fill your kitchen with the comfy-cozy aroma of freshly baked apples. To add to the homey look, you can try cutting decorative slits in the pie's "lid" before baking.

Preheat the oven to 425°F.

Roll each piece of dough into an 11" circle. Place one crust in a 9" pie plate. Firmly press the dough against the bottom and sides of the pan.

Grate the peel from the lemon into a large bowl. Cut the lemon in half and squeeze the juice into the bowl. Discard the lemon. Add the apples, flour, ¾ cup of the brown sugar, and the cinnamon; toss to coat well. Spoon into the prepared crust.

Place the second crust over the pie filling. Fold both edges of the dough under and crimp the crust. Brush with the egg and sprinkle with the remaining 1 teaspoon brown sugar. Using a sharp knife, make slits in the top.

Bake for 10 minutes. Rotate the pie and reduce the oven temperature to 350°F. Bake for 60 minutes, or until the crust is golden brown and the fruit is bubbling. To prevent over-browning, cover the edge of the crust with foil if necessary during the last 15 to 20 minutes of baking. Cool on a rack for at least 2 hours.

Makes 10 servings

Per serving: 454 calories, 6 g protein, 63 g carbohydrates, 21 g fat, 48 mg cholesterol, 3 g fiber, 131 mg sodium

Spiced Apple Crumb Pie

Crust

1   recipe Basic Pie Crust
    (see tip on page 42)

Topping

¾   cup unbleached all-
    purpose flour
¼   cup packed brown sugar
¼   teaspoon ground
    cinnamon
⅛   teaspoon ground nutmeg
2   tablespoons butter

Filling

6   Granny Smith apples,
    peeled, cored, and sliced
    (about 8 cups)
1   tablespoon lemon juice
½   cup sugar
2½ tablespoons quick-
    cooking tapioca
½   teaspoon ground
    cinnamon

No one can resist the allure of a buttery sweet crumb topping complementing the wholesome goodness of sweet-and-tangy Granny Smith apples. This is a pie you'll make again and again.

To make the crust: Preheat the oven to 425°F. Roll the dough out to an 11" circle. Place the dough in a 9" round pie plate. Firmly press the dough against the bottom and sides of the pan. Fold the edges under and crimp the crust.

To make the topping: Place the flour, brown sugar, cinnamon, and nutmeg in a medium bowl. Using your fingers, work the butter into the mixture until it resembles coarse crumbs.

To make the filling: In a large bowl, toss the apples with the lemon juice. In a small bowl, combine the sugar, tapioca, and cinnamon. Sprinkle over the apples and gently toss to coat. Spoon into the prepared crust. Sprinkle with the topping.

Bake for 10 minutes. Reduce the oven temperature to 350°F and bake for 60 minutes, or until golden brown. To prevent overbrowning, cover the edge of the crust with foil if necessary during the last 15 to 20 minutes of baking. Cool on a rack for at least 2 hours.

Makes 10 servings
Per serving: 335 calories, 4 g protein, 52 g carbohydrates, 13 g fat, 20 mg cholesterol, 2 g fiber, 86 mg sodium

Country Peach Pie

2   **recipes Basic Pie Crust (see tip on page 42)**

12   **medium peaches, peeled and sliced (6 cups)**

⅔   **cup sugar**

3   **tablespoons cornstarch**

1   **teaspoon lemon juice**

¼   **teaspoon ground nutmeg**

Baked fresh peaches bubble through an artful lattice top in this home-style pie. Top each serving with a scoop of vanilla ice cream for an added touch of country goodness.

Preheat the oven to 425°F.

Roll each piece of pie dough into an 11" circle. Place one crust in a 9" pie plate. Firmly press the dough against the bottom and sides of the pan.

In a large bowl, combine the peaches, sugar, cornstarch, lemon juice, and nutmeg. Place in the prepared crust.

Cut the second crust into strips about ½" wide. Cross the two longest strips over the center of the pie. Cover the top strip with another long strip. Fold back every other strip and lay the cross strips in place. Then return the folded-back strips to their original position. When all the strips are in place, trim off the excess overhang. Fold the bottom crust over the strips and crimp the crust.

Bake for 45 minutes, or until the filling bubbles and the crust is golden. To prevent overbrowning, cover the edge of the crust with foil if necessary during the last 15 to 20 minutes of baking. Cool on a rack for at least 2 hours.

Makes 10 servings

Per serving: 431 calories, 5 g protein, 58 g carbohydrates, 21 g fat, 26 mg cholesterol, 2 g fiber, 118 mg sodium

Pumpkin Pie

1 recipe Basic Pie Crust (see tip on page 42)
2 eggs
2 cups solid-pack canned pumpkin
1 can (12 ounces) evaporated milk
¾ cup firmly packed brown sugar
2 tablespoons rum or bourbon (optional)
1 teaspoon vanilla extract
1 teaspoon ground cinnamon
½ teaspoon ground ginger
½ teaspoon ground nutmeg
¼ teaspoon salt

Native Americans first introduced the American colonists to pumpkin, and this historic family-pleasing pie has been a mainstay on Thanksgiving Day tables ever since. The mild, sweet pumpkin is delicately contrasted with warm and spicy cinnamon, ginger, and nutmeg. Definitely a dessert to be thankful for.

Preheat the oven to 400°F.

Roll the pie dough out to an 11" circle. Place the dough in a 9" pie plate. Firmly press the dough against the bottom and sides of the pan. Fold the edges under and crimp the crust.

Whisk the eggs in a large bowl. Whisk in the pumpkin, evaporated milk, brown sugar, rum or bourbon (if using), vanilla extract, cinnamon, ginger, nutmeg, and salt until well-blended. Place the filling in the prepared crust.

Bake for 10 minutes. Reduce the oven temperature to 350°F and bake for 40 minutes, or until the crust is browned and the filling is just set in the center. To prevent over-browning, cover the edge of the crust with foil if necessary during the last 15 to 20 minutes of baking. Cool on a rack for at least 2 hours. Chill in the refrigerator until ready to serve.

Makes 10 servings
Per serving: 303 calories, 6 g protein, 39 g carbohydrates, 14 g fat, 66 mg cholesterol, 2 g fiber, 175 mg sodium

Phyllo Lemon Meringue Pie

8   sheets phyllo dough (13"
x 9" each), thawed
according to package
directions

1½ cups water

6   tablespoons cornstarch

1¼ cups sugar, divided

½   cup lemon juice

4   egg yolks

2   teaspoons grated lemon
peel

6   egg whites, at room
temperature

⅛   teaspoon cream of tartar

½   teaspoon vanilla extract

Here's the much-loved cousin of popular Key Lime Pie (page 56). The fluffy meringue floats atop the sweetly tart filling—heaven on earth!

Preheat the oven to 350°F. Grease a 9" pie plate.

Drape 1 sheet of the phyllo dough across the plate. Press into the plate and fold the overhanging edges toward the center, crumpling them slightly to fit. Coat with cooking spray. Repeat layering and spraying with the remaining sheets of phyllo. Bake for 20 minutes, or until the shell is golden brown. Cool on a rack.

In a medium saucepan, whisk the water and cornstarch until the cornstarch is dissolved. Whisk in 1 cup of the sugar and the lemon juice. Cook over medium-high heat, whisking constantly, for 5 minutes, or until the mixture comes to a boil. Continue whisking until clear and thick.

Remove from the heat and gradually whisk in the egg yolks. Return to medium heat and cook, whisking constantly, for 2 minutes, or until thickened. Whisk in the lemon peel. Set aside to cool to room temperature.

Place the egg whites in a large bowl. With an electric mixer on medium speed, beat until foamy. Add the cream of tartar and vanilla extract and beat until soft peaks form. Beat in the remaining ¼ cup sugar, 1 tablespoon at a time, until stiff, glossy peaks form.

Spoon the cooled lemon filling into the cooled crust. Spread the meringue over the pie to cover the filling and touch the crust. Make peaks in the meringue with a spoon.

Bake for 6 minutes, or until the meringue is golden brown. Cool on a rack for at least 2 hours. Cover and refrigerate until serving.

Makes 8 servings

Per serving: 243 calories, 5 g protein, 47 g carbohydrates, 4 g fat, 106 mg cholesterol, 1 g fiber, 139 mg sodium

Creamy Chocolate Mousse Pie

1½ cups chocolate cookie
crumbs

⅓ cup sugar

⅓ cup butter, melted

2½ cups half-and-half

2 packages (4-serving size
each) instant chocolate
pudding and pie filling

½ cup heavy cream

1 teaspoon vanilla extract

This fluffy treat is a hit with adults and kids alike. And it's a snap to change the filling to fit your taste cravings—all you have to do is use different flavors of pudding mix.

Preheat the oven to 375°F.

In a 9" pie plate, combine the cookie crumbs and sugar. Add the butter and stir until well blended. Press the crumb mixture firmly into the bottom and up the sides of the plate. Bake for 6 minutes. Cool completely on a rack before filling.

In a large bowl, whisk together the half-and-half and the pudding mix for 2 minutes, or until smooth and creamy.

In a small bowl, with an electric mixer on medium-high speed, beat the heavy cream until soft peaks form. Fold into the pudding mixture along with the vanilla extract.

Spoon into the prepared crust. Cover and refrigerate for at least 3 hours.

Makes 10 servings

Per serving: 344 calories, 3 g protein, 40 g carbohydrates, 20 g fat, 57 mg cholesterol, 1 g fiber, 524 mg sodium

Classic Key Lime Pie

1½ cups finely crushed gingersnap cookies

⅓ cup sugar

⅓ cup butter, melted

½ cup Key lime juice or fresh lime juice

1 can (14 ounces) sweetened condensed milk

2 egg yolks

1 tablespoon grated lime peel

½ cup sugar

1 teaspoon cornstarch

4 egg whites

¼ teaspoon cream of tartar

Grown in the Florida Keys, Key limes have more intense flavor than regular limes. Look for Key lime juice in the international aisle of your supermarket.

Preheat the oven to 375°F.

In a 9" pie plate, combine the cookie crumbs, sugar, and butter. Press the crumb mixture firmly into the bottom and up the sides of the plate. Bake for 6 minutes, or until just beginning to brown. Cool completely on a rack before filling.

In a large bowl, combine the lime juice, condensed milk, egg yolks, and lime peel.

In a small bowl, stir together the sugar and cornstarch.

Place the egg whites and cream of tartar in another medium bowl. With an electric mixer on medium speed, beat until foamy. Increase the speed to high and gradually beat in the sugar mixture until stiff glossy peaks form.

Fold ¾ cup of the meringue into the lime mixture. Place in the prepared crust and bake for 15 minutes. Remove from the oven; reduce the oven temperature to 350°F.

Spread the remaining meringue over the pie so that it covers the filling and touches the crust around the edge. Bake for 10 minutes, or until the meringue is golden brown and set. Cool on a rack for at least 2 hours. Cover and refrigerate.

Makes 10 servings

Per serving: 333 calories, 6 g protein, 51 g carbohydrates, 12 g fat, 73 mg cholesterol, 0 g fiber, 240 mg sodium

Rich Peanut Butter Pie

1½ cups chocolate cookie crumbs

⅓ cup sugar

⅓ cup butter, melted

½ cup + ¼ cup heavy cream

8 ounces cream cheese, softened

¾ cup creamy peanut butter

¾ cup confectioners' sugar

2 tablespoons butter, softened

2 tablespoons vanilla extract

3 tablespoons chocolate chips

This creamy, rich pie is actually quite airy and light. It's perfect for peanut butter lovers, as well as those who just have an incurable sweet tooth.

Preheat the oven to 375°F.

In a 9" pie plate, combine the cookie crumbs and sugar. Add the butter and stir until well blended. Press the crumb mixture firmly into the bottom and up the sides of the plate. Bake for 6 minutes. Cool completely on a rack before filling.

In a small bowl, with an electric mixer on medium-high speed, beat ½ cup of the heavy cream until soft peaks form.

In a medium bowl, with an electric mixer and the same beaters on medium speed, beat the cream cheese, peanut butter, confectioners' sugar, butter, and vanilla extract until well-blended.

Fold the whipped cream into the peanut butter mixture. Spread evenly in the prepared crust. Chill for at least 1 hour.

Meanwhile, in a small saucepan over medium heat, melt the chocolate chips along with the remaining ¼ cup heavy cream, stirring constantly, until smooth. Drizzle in a decorative pattern over the chilled pie.

Makes 12 servings

Per serving: 393 calories, 7 g protein, 27 g carbohydrates, 30 g fat, 62 mg cholesterol, 1 g fiber, 297 mg sodium

Chocolate Pecan Pie

1 recipe Basic Pie Crust (see tip on page 42)

1½ cups pecan halves

2 tablespoons butter

½ cup firmly packed brown sugar

1 cup dark corn syrup

3 eggs, lightly beaten

1½ teaspoons cornstarch

4 ounces semisweet chocolate, melted

1–2 tablespoons bourbon

No dessert seems more opulent than Southern pecan pie, generously topped with whipped cream. This version does not disappoint, with plenty of pecans to provide the buttery richness.

Preheat the oven to 375°F. Roll the pie dough out to a 13" circle. Place the dough in a 9" pie plate. Firmly press the dough against the bottom and sides of the pan. Fold the edges under and crimp the crust. Chop 1 cup of the pecan halves and place in the bottom of the crust. Reserve the remaining ½ cup pecan halves.

In a medium bowl, with an electric mixer on medium speed, beat the butter, brown sugar, and corn syrup until well-blended. Beat in the eggs and cornstarch. While beating, slowly drizzle in the chocolate and beat until blended. Beat in the bourbon. Place over the pecans in the pie crust. Carefully arrange the remaining ½ cup pecan halves over the pie, pressing them gently with a fork to coat with filling.

Bake for 45 minutes, or until a knife inserted near the center comes out clean. Cool on a rack.

Makes 10 servings
Per serving: 362 calories, 4 g protein, 48 g carbohydrates, 19 g fat, 70 mg cholesterol, 2 g fiber, 72 mg sodium

Spirited Pecan Tart

1   recipe Basic Tart Crust (see tip)
2   eggs, lightly beaten
1   cup sugar
⅔   cup light corn syrup
1   tablespoon rum or bourbon
1   tablespoon butter, melted
1   tablespoon unbleached all-purpose flour
½   teaspoon vanilla extract
1   cup pecan halves
1   cup chopped pecans

What an inventive twist on prized pecan pie. Here, a flaky tart crust couches a syrupy filling and crunchy pecans. Simply divine.

Preheat the oven to 350°F.

Roll the dough out to a 12" circle. Place the dough in an 11" tart pan. Firmly press the dough against the bottom and sides of the pan. Trim the edges.

In a medium bowl, whisk together the eggs, sugar, corn syrup, rum or bourbon, butter, flour, and vanilla extract. Place into the prepared crust. Arrange the pecan halves over the filling in 2 rows around the outside edge of the tart. Place the chopped pecans in the middle of the tart, sprinkling them to meet the edge of the pecan halves.

Bake for 45 minutes, or until browned and the center is set. Cool on a rack for at least 2 hours.

Makes 12 servings

Per serving: 389 calories, 5 g protein, 47 g carbohydrates, 22 g fat, 49 mg cholesterol, 2 g fiber, 91 mg sodium

COOKING TIP

To make an 11" Basic Tart Crust, in a large bowl, combine 1½ cups unbleached all-purpose flour, 2 tablespoons sugar, and ¼ teaspoon salt. Cut in ¼ cup unsalted butter and ¼ cup vegetable shortening until the mixture resembles coarse crumbs. Sprinkle 2 to 4 tablespoons ice water over the crumbs and toss with a fork until the dough holds together. Gather the mixture into a ball and press into a thick disk. Cover and refrigerate for 15 to 30 minutes before rolling out. Bake as directed.

Spirited Pecan Tart on page 59

Delicate Pear Tart

1   recipe Basic Tart Crust
    (see tip on page 59)
    prepared adding ½
    teaspoon ground
    cinnamon to the flour
    mixture

6   ripe medium pears,
    peeled, cored, halved,
    and thinly sliced

¼   cup packed brown sugar

⅓   cup chopped walnuts

¼   cup apple jelly

A flower-shaped tart pan lets you shape the dough into a lovely design, but a round tart pan will work just as well. Here, some of the pears are grouped in the center to create a fruity "flower."

Preheat the oven to 350°F.

Roll the tart dough out to an 11" circle. Place the dough in a 9½" flower tart pan or a 10" tart pan. Firmly press the dough against the bottom and sides of the pan. Trim the edges. Arrange the pears in the crust in a decorative pattern. Sprinkle with the brown sugar and walnuts. Bake for 45 minutes, or until the pears are tender and the pastry is golden. Cool on a rack for 10 minutes. Brush with the jelly. Cool on a rack for at least 2 hours.

Makes 12 servings
Per serving: 247 calories, 3 g protein, 36 g carbohydrates, 11 g fat, 11 mg cholesterol, 2 g fiber, 53 mg sodium

Peach 'n' Pudding Tart

1 recipe Basic Tart Crust (see tip on page 59)
1 cup milk
1 package (4-serving size) French vanilla instant pudding and pie filling
8 ounces sour cream
¼ teaspoon almond extract
3 ripe medium peaches, thinly sliced
2 tablespoons apple jelly, melted

This fancy looking tart is really quite easy to make. The pudding mix is the secret to whipping up a quick, custardlike filling that makes a creamy cushion for juicy sliced peaches.

Preheat the oven to 425°F.

Roll the dough out to a 12" circle. Place the dough in an 11" tart pan. Firmly press the dough against the bottom and sides of the pan. Trim the edges. Using a fork, pierce the bottom of the crust all over. Bake for 10 minutes, or until lightly browned. Cool completely on a rack.

Meanwhile, in a large bowl, whisk together the milk and pudding mix for 2 minutes, or until smooth and creamy. Whisk in the sour cream and almond extract until smooth.

Place into the cooled crust and smooth the top. Arrange the peaches over the filling, overlapping in a circular pattern. Brush the peaches with the jelly. Refrigerate for at least 2 hours.

Makes 12 servings
Per serving: 246 calories, 3 g protein, 29 g carbohydrates, 13 g fat, 22 mg cholesterol, 1 g fiber, 190 mg sodium

Chocolate Banana Tart

1   recipe Basic Tart Crust (see tip on page 59)

½   cup + 1 tablespoon mini semisweet chocolate chips

4   egg yolks

½   cup sugar

⅓   cup unbleached all-purpose flour

¼   teaspoon salt

2   cups heavy cream

1   ripe banana, mashed

A creamy banana pudding fills this chocolate-lined tart shell. Dolloped with whipped cream, this elegant tart is sure to please.

Preheat the oven to 425°F.

Roll the dough out to a 12" circle. Place the dough in an 11" tart pan. Firmly press the dough against the bottom and sides of the pan. Trim the edges. Using a fork, pierce the bottom of the crust all over. Bake for 16 minutes, or until lightly browned. Sprinkle with ½ cup of the chocolate chips, spreading to melt and coat the bottom of the crust. Cool completely on a rack.

In a medium bowl, beat the egg yolks. In a medium saucepan, combine the sugar, flour, and salt. Whisk in 1½ cups of the cream, bring to a simmer, and cook, stirring frequently, over medium heat for 8 minutes, or until the mixture has thickened. Remove the pan from the heat.

Slowly whisk about 1 cup of the hot cream mixture into the egg yolks. Whisk back into the cream mixture and cook, whisking constantly, for 2 minutes, or until thickened. Place the mixture in a medium bowl and cover with a piece of waxed paper or plastic wrap. Refrigerate for 20 minutes, or until chilled and slightly firm. Fold the banana into the mixture and place in the prepared crust.

Meanwhile, in a medium bowl, with an electric mixer on medium speed, beat the remaining ½ cup cream until soft peaks form. Garnish the tart with the whipped cream and remaining 1 tablespoon chocolate chips.

Makes 12 servings

Per serving: 409 calories, 5 g protein, 36 g carbohydrates, 29 g fat, 137 mg cholesterol, 1 g fiber, 116 mg sodium

Caramel Apple Tart

1   **recipe Basic Tart Crust (see tip on page 59)**

1   **egg**

3   **tablespoons butter**

5   **tablespoons packed brown sugar**

½   **cup heavy cream**

½   **teaspoon vanilla extract**

¼   **teaspoon ground cinnamon**

     Pinch of salt

6   **Granny Smith apples, peeled, cored, and thickly sliced (about 8 cups)**

⅓   **cup walnuts, finely chopped**

If you like caramel apples, you'll love this tart. Here, the apples are caramelized in brown sugar and cream to create a treat that is sweetly sublime.

Preheat the oven to 425°F.

Roll the dough out to a 12" circle. Place the dough in the prepared tart pan. Firmly press the dough against the bottom and sides of the pan. Trim the edges. Using a fork, pierce the bottom of the crust all over. Bake for 12 minutes, or until lightly browned. Cool on a rack. Reduce the oven temperature to 350°F.

Meanwhile, in a small bowl, beat the egg. In a large skillet over medium-high heat, cook the butter, brown sugar, and cream for 5 minutes, or until slightly thickened. Slowly whisk about ¼ cup of the cream mixture into the beaten egg. Whisk back into the cream mixture and cook, whisking constantly, for 4 minutes, or until caramel in color. Stir in the vanilla extract, cinnamon, and salt. Add the apples and cook, turning frequently, for 5 minutes, or until coated. Place the apple mixture in the prepared crust and sprinkle with the walnuts. Bake for 55 minutes, or until browned.

Makes 12 servings

Per serving: 151 calories, 2 g protein, 17 g carbohydrates, 9 g fat, 40 mg cholesterol, 2 g fiber, 73 mg sodium

Orchard Plum Tart

1   recipe Basic Tart Crust (see tip on page 59) prepared adding ¼ teaspoon ground cinnamon to the flour mixture

⅓   cup almond paste

6   plums, quartered and pitted

1   tablespoon milk

1   tablespoon sugar

2   tablespoons red currant jelly

Mouth-watering juicy plums make a dazzling appearance in this simple yet stunning dessert. The red currant jelly sneaks in at the very end to give the fruit an eye-catching glaze.

Preheat oven to 400°F.

Roll the dough out to a 12" circle. Place on a baking sheet.

Spread the almond paste over the dough, leaving a 1½" border around the edge. Arrange the plums in a decorative pattern over the almond paste. Fold the pastry border over the outside edge of the plums. Brush the milk over the pastry and sprinkle with the sugar.

Bake for 30 minutes, or until the crust is golden and the juices are bubbling. Cool on a rack for 10 minutes. Brush with the jelly. Cool on a rack for at least 2 hours.

To serve, using a long metal spatula, loosen the pastry and slide onto a serving platter.

Makes 10 servings

Per serving: 243 calories, 3 g protein, 30 g carbohydrates, 13 g fat, 13 mg cholesterol, 1 g fiber, 62 mg sodium

---

COOKING TIP

If fresh plums are not available, you can use 1 can (16 ounces) whole plums, drained.

Fruit-Studded Creme Tart

1   recipe Basic Tart Crust (see tip on page 59)
1   cup sugar
¼   cup + 2 tablespoons unbleached all-purpose flour
¼   teaspoon salt
2   cups milk
4   egg yolks
1½ teaspoons vanilla extract
2   cups assorted fresh fruit such as strawberries, raspberries, blueberries, peeled and sliced kiwifruit, sliced peaches, and/or sliced plums

A homemade vanilla pastry cream makes this tart special. Arrange the assorted fresh fruit in a decorative circular pattern for an impressive presentation.

Preheat the oven to 425°F.

Roll the dough out to a 12" circle. Place the dough in an 11" tart pan. Firmly press the dough against the bottom and sides of the pan. Trim the edges. Using a fork, pierce the bottom of the crust all over. Bake for 12 minutes, or until lightly browned. Cool completely on a rack.

In a medium bowl, combine the sugar, flour, and salt.

In a small saucepan over medium-high heat, heat the milk until hot but not boiling. Remove from the heat and stir in the sugar mixture. Return to the heat and cook, stirring constantly, for 4 minutes, or until thick and smooth. Add the egg yolks and cook, stirring, for 2 minutes longer. Remove from the heat and cool slightly, stirring occasionally. Stir in the vanilla extract. Place into the prepared crust and spread evenly. Cool on a rack for 2 hours.

Arrange the fruit on top of the custard. Serve immediately or refrigerate until ready to serve.

Makes 10 servings
Per serving: 331 calories, 6 g protein, 46 g carbohydrates, 14 g fat, 105 mg cholesterol, 1 g fiber, 145 mg sodium

Double Chocolate Tart

1   recipe Basic Tart Crust (see tip on page 59)
1   cup semisweet chocolate chips
2   egg yolks
½   cup sugar
2   tablespoons cornstarch
    Pinch of salt
3   cups milk
4   ounces good-quality white chocolate, finely chopped
1   tablespoon butter
1   tablespoon raspberry liqueur (optional)
1   teaspoon vanilla extract
    Fresh raspberries for garnish
    Chocolate curls for garnish

Raspberry liqueur and vanilla extract blend with a blanket of satiny white chocolate, layered upon a semisweet chocolate laced crust to create a taste that will make you swoon with delight. And what better way to top it off than with a scattering of fresh raspberries?

Preheat the oven to 425°F.

Roll the dough out to a 12" circle. Place the dough in an 11" tart pan. Firmly press the dough against the bottom and sides of the pan. Trim the edges. Using a fork, pierce the bottom of the crust all over. Bake for 12 minutes, or until lightly browned. Sprinkle with the chocolate chips, spreading to melt and coat the bottom of the crust. Cool completely on a rack.

In a medium bowl, beat the egg yolks. In a medium saucepan, combine the sugar, cornstarch, and salt. Whisk in the milk until well blended. Add the white chocolate. Place over medium-high heat and cook, whisking constantly, for 8 minutes, or until the chocolate has melted and the mixture is thickened. Remove from the heat.

Slowly whisk 1 cup hot chocolate mixture into the egg yolks. Whisk back into the pan and cook, whisking constantly, for 2 minutes, or until thick. Remove from the heat and stir in the butter, liqueur (if using), and vanilla extract. Place in a medium bowl and cover with a piece of waxed paper or plastic wrap. Refrigerate for 20 minutes, or until chilled and slightly firm.

Place the chilled chocolate mixture in the prepared crust. Garnish with raspberries and chocolate curls.

Makes 12 servings
Per serving: 358 calories, 6 g protein, 41 g carbohydrates, 20 g fat, 59 mg cholesterol, 1 g fiber, 134 mg sodium

Sunshine Lemon Tart

1   recipe Basic Tart Crust (see tip on page 59)
4   eggs
½   cup sugar
1½ cups half-and-half
⅓   cup freshly squeezed lemon juice
1   teaspoon grated lemon peel
1   teaspoon vanilla extract
    Lemon slices for garnish (optional)

A bright yellow tart topped with fresh lemons looks just like a burst of summer sunshine. Your tastebuds will awaken to the tangy punch of citrus.

Preheat the oven to 425°F.

Roll the tart dough out to a 12" circle. Place the dough in the prepared tart pan. Firmly press the dough against the bottom and sides of the pan. Trim the edges. Using a fork, pierce the bottom of the crust all over. Bake for 12 minutes, or until lightly browned. Cool on a rack.

Reduce the oven temperature to 325°F.

In large bowl, whisk the eggs until fluffy. Add the sugar and stir until thick. Stir in the half-and-half, lemon juice, lemon peel, and vanilla extract just until combined.

Place the cooled crust on a baking sheet. Place the filling in the crust. Bake for 1 hour, or until the filling is set and a knife inserted in the center comes out clean. To prevent over-browning, cover the edge of the crust with foil if necessary during the last 15 to 20 minutes of baking. Cool on a rack for at least 2 hours. Arrange the lemon slices over the tart, if desired. Cover and refrigerate until serving.

Makes 12 servings
Per serving: 240 calories, 5 g protein, 25 g carbohydrates, 14 g fat, 93 mg cholesterol, 0 g fiber, 83 mg sodium

Peach Clafouti

1 teaspoon butter, softened

1 teaspoon + ½ cup granulated sugar

1⅓ cups milk

¾ cup unbleached all-purpose flour

3 eggs

1 teaspoon vanilla extract

2 tablespoons minced crystallized ginger

⅛ teaspoon salt

3 cups sliced fresh peaches (about 4 medium peaches)

2 tablespoons + 2 teaspoons confectioners' sugar

A clafouti is made with fresh fruit topped by a pastry batter. Serve as a dessert or as a fancy feature at a brunch.

Preheat the oven to 400°F. Coat a 9" deep-dish pie plate or quiche pan with the butter, then sprinkle with 1 teaspoon of the granulated sugar.

In a large bowl, whisk together the milk, flour, the remaining ½ cup granulated sugar, eggs, vanilla extract, ginger, and salt until well-mixed.

Place half of the batter into the prepared pie plate.

In a medium bowl, combine the peaches and 2 tablespoons of the confectioners' sugar. Arrange the peaches in a pattern over the batter. Top with the remaining batter. Bake for 50 minutes, or until the clafouti is puffed, browned, and firm. Cool on a rack for at least 20 minutes.

To serve, sprinkle with the remaining 2 teaspoons confectioners' sugar.

Makes 8 servings
Per serving: 203 calories, 5 g protein, 37 g carbohydrates, 4 g fat, 87 mg cholesterol, 1 g fiber, 97 mg sodium

Cherry-Almond Clafouti

1   teaspoon butter, softened

1   teaspoon + ½ cup granulated sugar

1⅓ cups milk

¾   cup unbleached all-purpose flour

3   eggs

¼   teaspoon almond extract

2   cups pitted sweet cherries

1½ teaspoons confectioners' sugar

A classic French favorite, this clafouti uses the traditional cherry topping. You can substitute thawed frozen cherries if fresh aren't available.

Preheat the oven to 400°F. Coat a 9" deep-dish pie plate or quiche pan with the butter and dust with 1 teaspoon of the granulated sugar.

In a large bowl, whisk together the milk, flour, the remaining ½ cup granulated sugar, eggs, and almond extract until well-blended.

Place half of the batter into the prepared pie plate. Add the cherries, then top with the remaining batter.

Bake for 40 minutes, or until the clafouti is puffed, browned, and firm. Cool on a rack for at least 20 minutes.

To serve, sprinkle with the confectioners' sugar.

Makes 6 servings

Per serving: 177 calories, 6 g protein, 30 g carbohydrates, 4 g fat, 87 mg cholesterol, 1 g fiber, 49 mg sodium

---

COOKING TIP

If you don't have a cherry pitter, you can use a paper clip to pit the cherries. Unfold one end of a large paper clip and use the "hook" to remove the pit.

SUPER-SIMPLE PUDDINGS, CUSTARDS, AND FOOLS

Simple Chocolate Pudding

2   egg yolks
½   cup sugar
2   tablespoons cornstarch
⅛   teaspoon salt
2   cups milk
4   ounces bittersweet or semisweet chocolate, finely chopped
1   tablespoon butter, softened
1   teaspoon vanilla extract
4   chocolate wafer cookies, crushed
     Fresh raspberries for garnish

Chocolate pudding is always a welcome treat. Here, bittersweet chocolate provides a deep richness that makes this version extra-special, and the dusting of cookie crumbs adds crunchy contrast. To vary the presentation, dunk a whole chocolate cookie into each serving.

In a medium bowl, beat the egg yolks.

In a medium saucepan, combine the sugar, cornstarch, and salt. Whisk in the milk and add the chocolate. Bring to a boil and cook, stirring frequently, over medium heat for 8 minutes, or until the chocolate is melted and the pudding has thickened. Remove the pan from the heat.

Slowly whisk about 1 cup of the hot pudding mixture into the egg yolks. Whisk back into the pudding and cook, whisking constantly, for 2 minutes, or until the pudding has thickened.

Remove the pan from the heat and stir in the butter and vanilla extract. Place the pudding in a bowl and cover with a piece of waxed paper or plastic wrap on the surface of the pudding. Refrigerate for 1 hour, or until chilled.

To serve, spoon the pudding into dessert dishes. Dust with the cookie crumbs and top with raspberries.

Makes 4 servings
Per serving: 409 calories, 8 g protein, 54 g carbohydrates, 20 g fat, 132 mg cholesterol, 2 g fiber, 236 mg sodium

Hearty Rice Pudding

1½ cups water
¾ cup uncooked rice
¼ teaspoon salt
2 cups half-and-half
1 cup milk
½ cup + 1 teaspoon sugar
1 teaspoon vanilla extract
½ pint fresh raspberries

Your family will love the creamy texture and comforting mild flavor of this soothing dessert. The raspberry sauce dresses things up and contributes a lovely smooth sweetness.

In a medium saucepan, combine the water, rice, and salt and bring to a boil over high heat. Reduce the heat to low, cover, and simmer for 20 minutes, or until the rice is tender and the liquid is absorbed. Stir in the half-and-half, milk, and ½ cup of the sugar. Simmer, uncovered, stirring frequently, for 25 minutes, or until the mixture begins to thicken. Reduce the heat to medium-low and cook, stirring frequently, for 20 minutes, or until thickened. Stir in the vanilla extract. Cool for 10 minutes to serve warm. Or, place in a bowl, cover with a piece of waxed paper or plastic wrap, and refrigerate for at least 3 hours.

Reserve half of the raspberries for garnish. In a blender, puree the remaining raspberries. Strain to remove the seeds and sweeten with the remaining 1 teaspoon sugar.

To serve, spoon the pudding into dessert dishes, drizzle with raspberry sauce, and top with the remaining raspberries.

Makes 8 servings
Per serving: 219 calories, 4 g protein, 32 g carbohydrates, 9 g fat, 26 mg cholesterol, 2 g fiber, 115 mg sodium

French Vanilla Pudding

2   egg yolks
½   cup sugar
2   tablespoons cornstarch
⅛   teaspoon salt
2   cups milk
½   vanilla bean, split lengthwise in half
2   tablespoons butter, softened

You may not think that a pudding can be decadent, but one taste of this fantastic flavor, and you'll see that the proof is in the pudding! A simple vanilla bean is the magic in the mix.

In a medium bowl, beat the egg yolks.

In a medium saucepan, combine the sugar, cornstarch, and salt. Whisk in the milk and add the vanilla bean. Bring to a boil and cook, stirring frequently, over medium heat for 10 minutes, or until the pudding has thickened. Remove the pan from the heat.

Remove the vanilla bean and scrape the seeds back into the pan. Discard the bean. Slowly whisk about 1 cup of the hot pudding mixture into the egg yolks. Whisk back into the pan and cook, whisking constantly, for 2 minutes, or until the pudding has thickened. Stir in the butter.

Place the pudding in a bowl and cover with a piece of waxed paper or plastic wrap on the surface of the pudding. Refrigerate for 1 hour, or until chilled.

Makes 4 servings
Per serving: 270 calories, 5 g protein, 34 g carbohydrates, 13 g fat, 139 mg cholesterol, 0 g fiber, 219 mg sodium

Crème Caramel

3 tablespoons water
1¼ cups sugar
1 cup milk
1 cup light cream
4 eggs
1 teaspoon vanilla extract

Crème caramel, also called flan, is a custard that's baked in a dish lined with caramel. A distinctive dessert for an elegant end to any meal.

Preheat the oven to 350°F. Place six 4-ounce custard cups in a baking dish.

In a medium saucepan over medium-high heat, combine the water and ¾ cup of the sugar. Cook, stirring, for 1 minute, or until the sugar is dissolved. Cover the pan, bring to a boil, and cook for 3 minutes, or until the bubbles are thick. Uncover, reduce the heat to medium, and cook, without stirring, for 2 minutes, or until the syrup darkens to a medium amber color. Immediately pour the syrup into the custard cups and swirl to coat the bottoms and halfway up the sides.

In another medium saucepan over medium heat, combine the milk, cream, and the remaining ½ cup sugar. Cook, stirring occasionally, until just to the boiling point. Remove from the heat.

Whisk the eggs in a large bowl. Slowly whisk in the milk mixture. Stir in the vanilla extract, then strain the mixture through a sieve and pour into the custard cups.

Fill the baking dish with ½" warm water and cover with foil. Bake for 30 minutes, or until the custards are just set.

Remove from the oven and water bath. Cool on a rack for 15 minutes, then refrigerate for at least 1 hour to chill. Let stand at room temperature for 1 hour before serving. Just before serving, run a knife around the edge of each serving and invert onto a plate.

Makes 6 servings
Per serving: 310 calories, 7 g protein, 44 g carbohydrates, 12 g fat, 174 mg cholesterol, 0 g fiber, 78 mg sodium

Lemon-Scented Bread Pudding

8   ounces French or Italian bread, cut into cubes (5½ cups)

1½ cups light cream

½   cup sugar

1   tablespoon lemon peel

3   eggs

1   teaspoon vanilla extract

Fresh raspberries and/or blueberries

This old-time classic has been around for generations. It's a tasty, creative way to use last night's leftover bread.

Grease a 9" x 5" loaf pan. Place the bread in the prepared pan.

In a small saucepan over low heat, combine the cream, sugar, and lemon peel. Cook, stirring occasionally, until the sugar is dissolved. Remove from the heat and let stand for 15 minutes.

In a large bowl, whisk together the eggs and vanilla extract. Slowly whisk in the cream mixture. Pour over the bread and press down lightly to make sure that all of the bread is moistened. Cover and refrigerate for 2 hours.

Preheat the oven to 350°F. Uncover the bread pudding and press down lightly on the bread to coat with filling. Bake for 35 minutes, or until slightly puffed and set. If the top browns too quickly, cover with foil during the last 15 minutes of baking time. Cool on a rack for at least 20 minutes. Serve warm or cover and refrigerate for at least 3 hours. Serve with the berries.

Makes 8 servings

Per serving: 249 calories, 6 g protein, 31 g carbohydrates, 12 g fat, 109 mg cholesterol, 2 g fiber, 214 mg sodium

Chocolate Bread Pudding

8   ounces French or Italian
     bread, cut into cubes
     (about 5½ cups)
1   cup heavy cream
1   cup milk
6   ounces semisweet
     chocolate, chopped
3   eggs
⅔   cup packed brown sugar
1   teaspoon vanilla extract
¼   teaspoon salt
1   tablespoon
     confectioners' sugar

You'll love the richness of semisweet chocolate in this dense bread pudding. Make it even more sinful by serving warm with softly whipped cream.

Grease an 8" x 8" baking dish. Place the bread cubes in the prepared baking dish.

In a medium saucepan over low heat, combine the heavy cream, milk, and chocolate. Cook, stirring occasionally, for 10 minutes, or until the chocolate is melted. Remove from the heat.

In a large bowl, whisk together the eggs, brown sugar, vanilla extract, and salt. Slowly whisk in the chocolate mixture. Pour over the bread cubes and press down lightly to make sure that all of the bread is moistened. Cover and refrigerate for 2 hours.

Preheat the oven to 350°F. Uncover the pudding and press down lightly on the bread cubes to coat with filling. Bake for 35 minutes, or until slightly puffed and set. If the top browns too quickly, cover with foil near the end of baking time. Cool on a rack for at least 20 minutes. Serve warm or cover and refrigerate for at least 3 hours. Just before serving, sift the confectioners' sugar over the pudding.

Makes 8 servings

Per serving: 407 calories, 8 g protein, 48 g carbohydrates, 22 g fat, 125 mg cholesterol, 2 g fiber, 302 mg sodium

Sweet Noodle Pudding

1   **pound wide egg noodles**
¾   **cup butter**
1½ **cups cornflake crumbs**
½   **cup sugar**
2   **teaspoons ground cinnamon**
8   **ounces cream cheese, softened**
6   **eggs**
16 **ounces sour cream**
¾   **cup sugar**
1   **teaspoon vanilla extract**
1   **pound small-curd cottage cheese**
1   **can (20 ounces) crushed pineapple, drained**

A buttery, crunchy topping melts in your mouth as you savor the buttery noodles and custard. An excellent choice for a potluck supper or a dessert buffet. For a change of pace, substitute other chopped canned fruits for the pineapple.

Preheat the oven to 350°F. Grease a 13" x 9" baking pan. Prepare the noodles according to package directions.

Meanwhile, in a medium bowl, microwave ¼ cup butter on high for 2 minutes, or until melted. Cool slightly; stir in the cornflake crumbs, sugar, and cinnamon; set aside.

Drain the noodles and place in a large bowl. Add the cream cheese and the remaining ½ cup butter and stir until melted and the noodles are evenly coated.

Add the eggs, sour cream, sugar, and vanilla extract. Stir in the cottage cheese and pineapple and toss to coat well. Place in the prepared pan. Sprinkle with the cornflake mixture.

Bake for 45 minutes, or until the mixture is set. Cool on a rack for at least 20 minutes. Serve warm or cover and refrigerate for at least 3 hours.

Makes 18 servings
Per serving: 406 calories, 11 g protein, 44 g carbohydrates, 21 g fat, 144 mg cholesterol, 1 g fiber, 332 mg sodium

Tiramisu

2   **cups heavy cream**

¾   **cup sugar**

3   **egg yolks**

¼   **cup sweet Marsala**

8   **ounces mascarpone cheese, softened**

2   **packages (3 ounces each) ladyfingers**

¾   **cup hot instant espresso or strong brewed coffee**

½   **teaspoon unsweetened cocoa powder**

     Coffee beans for garnish (optional)

The creamy filling in this revered indulgence is a culinary classic beyond compare. Espresso-dipped ladyfingers contribute the freshly brewed flavor.

In a large bowl, beat the heavy cream with 2 tablespoons of the sugar until stiff peaks form. Set aside.

In the top of a double boiler over simmering water or in a large metal bowl placed over a saucepan of simmering water, whisk the egg yolks, ½ cup of the remaining sugar, and the Marsala for 8 minutes, or until thickened. Remove from the heat and beat with an electric mixer on medium speed until cool.

In a large bowl, with a rubber spatula, mash the cheese until smooth. Fold in the egg mixture, then half of the whipped cream.

Split the ladyfingers in half lengthwise. In a small bowl, combine the espresso and the remaining 2 tablespoons sugar and stir until the sugar is dissolved. Brush the espresso mixture on the cut side of the ladyfingers. Arrange the ladyfingers, dipped side in, around the sides of six 8-ounce dessert dishes. Evenly fill with the cheese mixture, then dollop each serving with the remaining whipped cream. Refrigerate for 1 hour, or until chilled.

Just before serving, sprinkle with the cocoa powder and garnish with coffee beans, if using.

Makes 8 servings

Per serving: 481 calories, 7 g protein, 33 g carbohydrates, 36 g fat, 271 mg cholesterol, 0 g fiber, 141 mg sodium

Strawberry-Banana Trifle

1   **package (16 ounces) fresh or frozen and thawed pound cake**

½   **cup Marsala**

1   **cup heavy cream**

2   **packages (4-serving size each) vanilla or French vanilla pudding and pie filling**

2   **cups milk**

1   **pint strawberries, hulled and halved**

3   **bananas, sliced diagonally**

Hailing from England, a trifle combines delicious custard with cake soaked in spirits. Traditional versions call for homemade custard and sponge cake, but this easy variation uses convenient pudding mix and pound cake.

With a serrated knife, cut the cake into 1" slices. Place the slices on a baking sheet and brush with the Marsala.

In a medium bowl, with an electric mixer on medium-high, beat the cream until stiff peaks form.

In a large bowl, using the same beaters, beat the pudding mix and milk, on low speed for 2 minutes, or until blended. Fold the whipped cream into the pudding mix.

Place one-third of the cake pieces in a large, straight-sided glass bowl. Spoon one-third of the pudding over the cake, followed by one-third of the strawberries, and one-third of the bananas. Repeat twice to use all the cake, pudding, and fruit. Cover and refrigerate for at least 2 hours.

Makes 10 servings

Per serving: 424 calories, 5 g protein, 54 g carbohydrates, 20 g fat, 90 mg cholesterol, 2 g fiber, 472 mg sodium

Classic Chocolate Soufflé

1   **tablespoon + ½ cup granulated sugar**

6   **ounces semisweet chocolate, chopped**

¼   **cup butter**

4   **egg whites**

4   **egg yolks**

⅓   **cup unbleached all-purpose flour**

1   **tablespoon vanilla extract**

    Confectioners' sugar for garnish

An irresistible mix of semisweet chocolate and butter makes an amazing splash in this light and airy dessert. A cooled soufflé will deflate a bit but tastes just as delicious.

Preheat the oven to 375°F. Grease six 6-ounce soufflé cups or ramekins and sprinkle with 1 tablespoon of the sugar. Set aside.

In a small saucepan over low heat, melt the chocolate and butter. Set aside to cool.

In a medium bowl, with an electric mixer on medium speed, beat the egg whites until foamy. Slowly add the remaining ½ cup granulated sugar and beat until stiff peaks form.

In a large bowl, whisk together the egg yolks, flour, and vanilla extract. Slowly whisk in the chocolate mixture. Stir in one-quarter of the egg white mixture, then gently fold in the remaining egg white mixture.

Evenly spoon into the prepared cups. Bake for 20 minutes, or until the soufflés are puffed and just set. Dust with the confectioners' sugar and serve immediately.

Makes 6 servings

Per serving: 365 calories, 7 g protein, 40 g carbohydrates, 21 g fat, 164 mg cholesterol, 2 g fiber, 124 mg sodium

Cappuccino Custard

2   egg yolks
½   cup sugar
2   tablespoons cornstarch
1   tablespoon instant
     espresso coffee granules
2   cups half-and-half
1   teaspoon vanilla extract
1   cup heavy cream
Ground cinnamon for garnish
Cocoa powder for garnish

Fluffy whipped cream plus velvety smooth coffee custard equals a whole new cup o' joe. The sprinkle of cinnamon and cocoa adds a contrasting warm sweetness.

In a medium bowl, whisk the egg yolks. In a medium saucepan over medium heat, combine the sugar, cornstarch, and espresso granules. Stir in the half-and-half. Bring to a boil and cook, stirring constantly, for 20 minutes, or until the mixture thickens.

Remove the pan from the heat and whisk about 1 cup of the custard mixture into the egg yolks. Whisk back into the pan and cook, stirring constantly, for 2 minutes, or until the custard has thickened. Stir in the vanilla extract. Place the pudding in a bowl and cover with a piece of waxed paper or plastic wrap on the surface of the pudding. Refrigerate for 30 minutes.

Meanwhile, in a small bowl, with an electric mixer on medium-high speed, beat the heavy cream until soft peaks form. Fold into the cooled custard. Pour into mugs or dessert cups and refrigerate for 1 hour, or until chilled. To serve, dust with the cinnamon and cocoa powder.

Makes 6 servings
Per serving: 338 calories, 4 g protein, 24 g carbohydrates, 26 g fat, 155 mg cholesterol, 0 g fiber, 51 mg sodium

Classic Crème Brûlée

1   **tablespoon butter, melted**

2   **cups light cream or half-and-half**

½   **cup granulated sugar**

1   **vanilla bean, split lengthwise**

6   **egg yolks**

4   **tablespoons packed brown sugar**

Crème brûlée is a chilled custard that is sprinkled with sugar and then placed under the broiler to create a hard glaze of caramelized sugar. What an intriguing combination of creamy and crunchy.

Preheat the oven to 300°F. Grease six ½-cup ramekins or custard cups with the butter. Place in a baking pan and set aside.

In a medium saucepan over medium heat, combine the cream or half-and-half, granulated sugar, and vanilla bean and cook, stirring occasionally, until the sugar is dissolved and the mixture just comes to a boil. Remove from the heat. Remove the vanilla bean and scrape the seeds back into the cream mixture. Discard the bean.

In a medium bowl, whisk the egg yolks until smooth. While whisking constantly, gradually add the cream mixture until well-blended. Evenly pour the custard into the prepared ramekins. Add warm water to the baking pan until it reaches halfway up the sides of the ramekins. Bake for 40 minutes, or until the custard is set in the center. Remove from the oven and water bath and cool to room temperature. Chill for at least 2 hours or overnight.

Preheat the broiler. Evenly spoon 2 teaspoons of the brown sugar over each ramekin. Place on a baking sheet and broil, rotating the baking sheet for even browning, until the brown sugar is melted and begins to brown, about 2 minutes. Refrigerate for 30 minutes, or until the custard is chilled and the topping has hardened.

Makes 6 servings

Per serving: 280 calories, 5 g protein, 29 g carbohydrates, 16 g fat, 248 mg cholesterol, 0 g fiber, 64 mg sodium

Caffé Crème Brûlée

1 tablespoon butter, melted

2 cups light cream or half-and-half

½ cup granulated sugar

2 tablespoons instant espresso coffee granules

1 tablespoon coffee-flavored liqueur

6 egg yolks

¼ cup chocolate coated coffee beans, crushed

Take classic crème brûlée and add a hint of delicious coffee flavor, and the result is a dark-roasted dream dessert. It's perfect served with crunchy almond biscotti.

Preheat the oven to 300°F. Grease six ½-cup ramekins or custard cups with the butter. Place in a baking pan and set aside.

In a medium saucepan over medium heat, combine the cream or half-and-half and granulated sugar and cook, stirring occasionally, until the sugar is dissolved and the mixture just comes to a boil. Remove from the heat. Stir in the espresso granules and liqueur until the espresso is dissolved.

In a medium bowl, whisk the egg yolks until smooth. While whisking constantly, gradually add the cream mixture until well-blended. Evenly pour the custard into the prepared ramekins. Add warm water to the baking pan until it reaches halfway up the sides of the ramekins. Bake for 30 minutes, or until the custard is set in the center. Remove from the oven and water bath and cool to room temperature. Chill for at least 2 hours or overnight.

Preheat the broiler. Evenly divide the crushed chocolate coated coffee beans over the custards. Place on a baking sheet and broil, rotating the baking sheet for even browning, until the chocolate is melted and begins to brown, about 2 minutes. Refrigerate for 30 minutes, or until the custard is chilled and the topping has hardened.

Makes 6 servings

Per serving: 263 calories, 6 g protein, 22 g carbohydrates, 17 g fat, 248 mg cholesterol, 0 g fiber, 63 mg sodium

Raspberry Crème Brûlée

1 tablespoon butter, melted

2 cups light cream or half-and-half

½ cup granulated sugar

6 egg yolks

1 tablespoon almond-flavored liqueur

1 pint fresh raspberries

¼ cup turbinado, Demerara, or granulated sugar (see tip)

Raspberries and almond liqueur blend beautifully in this fruity version of crème brûlée. If you like, drop additional fresh berries on top.

Preheat the oven to 300°F. Grease six ½-cup ramekins or custard cups with the butter. Place in a baking pan and set aside.

In a medium saucepan over medium heat, combine the cream or half-and-half and granulated sugar and cook, stirring occasionally, until the sugar is dissolved and the mixture just comes to a boil. Remove from the heat.

In a medium bowl, whisk the egg yolks until smooth. While whisking constantly, gradually add the cream mixture until well-blended. Stir in the liqueur and raspberries. Evenly pour the custard into the prepared ramekins. Add warm water to the baking pan until it reaches halfway up the sides of the ramekins. Bake for 40 minutes, or until the custard is set in the center. Remove from the oven and water bath and cool to room temperature. Chill for at least 2 hours or overnight.

Preheat the broiler. Evenly divide the golden sugar over each ramekin. Place on a baking sheet and broil, rotating the baking sheet for even browning, until the brown sugar is melted and begins to brown, about 2 minutes. Refrigerate for 30 minutes, or until the custard is chilled and the topping has hardened.

Makes 6 servings

Per serving: 303 calories, 6 g protein, 33 g carbohydrates, 17 g fat, 248 mg cholesterol, 3 g fiber, 61 mg sodium

---
COOKING TIP

Turbinado and Demerara sugar both have a natural golden color and a larger crystal than granulated sugar. Often sold as "raw sugar," turbinado has a slight molasses-like flavor, while Demerara has a hint of caramel flavor.

Mango Fool

3   **mangoes, peeled, pitted, and chopped**

½   **cup + 1 tablespoon confectioners' sugar**

1   **tablespoon orange liqueur**

1   **cup heavy cream**

Delicate, sweet mango blends with softly whipped cream in this cool summer dessert. Garnish with raspberries and mint sprigs for a lovely presentation.

Place the mangoes, ½ cup of the sugar, and the liqueur in a food processor and puree just until crushed.

In a medium bowl, with an electric mixer on medium speed, beat the cream and remaining 1 tablespoon sugar until soft peaks form. Gently fold the mango puree into the whipped cream just until blended. Serve immediately.

Makes 6 servings

Per serving: 282 calories, 1 g protein, 37 g carbohydrates, 15 g fat, 55 mg cholesterol, 2 g fiber, 17 mg sodium

Frozen Raspberry Fool

1 **package (12 ounces) frozen unsweetened raspberries**
¼ **cup confectioners' sugar**
½ **cup heavy cream**
½ **teaspoon vanilla extract**
   Fresh raspberries for garnish
   Mint sprigs for garnish

This simple frozen treat comes together in minutes—try varying the fruit for a different flavor combination.

In a food processor, process the frozen raspberries until finely shaved, scraping the bowl occasionally. With the machine running, add the sugar, cream, and vanilla extract and process 1 minute, or just until blended. Serve immediately with the fresh raspberries and mint.

Makes 4 servings

Per serving: 160 calories, 1 g protein, 15 g carbohydrates, 11 g fat, 41 mg cholesterol, 1 g fiber, 11 mg sodium

---

COOKING TIP

To make a lighter version of this dish, substitute 4 ounces of vanilla yogurt for the heavy cream.

Apple-Ginger Fool

2   cups applesauce

¼   cup + 1 tablespoon confectioners' sugar

1   tablespoon applejack or brandy (optional)

½   tablespoon minced crystallized ginger

1   cup heavy cream

Turn ordinary applesauce into a lovely dessert simply by tossing with whipped cream. The perfect last-minute treat.

In a small bowl, combine the applesauce, ¼ cup of the sugar, applejack or brandy (if using), and ginger.

In a medium bowl, with an electric mixer on medium speed, beat the cream and the remaining 1 tablespoon sugar until soft peaks form. Gently fold the applesauce mixture into the whipped cream just until blended. Serve immediately.

Makes 6 servings

Per serving: 286 calories, 1 g protein, 40 g carbohydrates, 15 g fat, 55 mg cholesterol, 1 g fiber, 19 mg sodium

IRRESISTIBLE CANNOLIS, CREPES, AND OTHER CONFECTIONS

Strawberry Crepes

8   prepared crepes
2   ounces cream cheese, softened
½   cup (4 ounces) sour cream
2   tablespoons + 1 tablespoon packed brown sugar
½   teaspoon grated lemon peel
¼   teaspoon vanilla extract
3   cups fresh strawberries, sliced

The image of elegance, crepes are always sure to impress. Ready-made crepes make preparation a snap—look for them in the produce section of your supermarket and whip together this almost-instant dessert during strawberry season.

Wrap the crepes in plastic wrap and microwave on high power for 1 minute.

In a medium bowl, with an electric mixer on medium speed, beat the cream cheese, sour cream, 2 tablespoons of the brown sugar, lemon peel, and vanilla extract until well-blended.

Evenly divide the cream cheese mixture among the crepes. Evenly divide 2 cups of the strawberries over the cheese mixture. Fold each crepe in half, then in half again. Arrange on a serving plate.

In a food processor or blender, puree ¾ cup of the remaining strawberries with the remaining 1 tablespoon brown sugar. Fold in the remaining ¼ cup strawberries. Drizzle the strawberry sauce over the crepes.

Makes 8 crepes
Per serving: 233 calories, 7 g protein, 24 g carbohydrates, 12 g fat, 116 mg cholesterol, 2 g fiber, 214 mg sodium

Chocolate-Cherry Cheese Crepes

Crepes

⅔ cup unbleached all-purpose flour

2 tablespoons unsweetened cocoa powder

2 tablespoons confectioners' sugar

¾ cup milk

2 eggs

1 tablespoon vegetable oil

Filling

16 ounces ricotta cheese

¾ cup confectioners' sugar

½ teaspoon vanilla extract

2 tablespoons of your favorite liqueur, such as amaretto or Grand Marnier

¼ cup dried cherries

½ cup cherry preserves, warmed

Making your own crepes at home allows you to keep some in stock for another day. To freeze any leftover crepes, stack them between pieces of waxed paper and tightly seal them in plastic wrap.

To make the crepes: In a medium bowl, combine the flour, cocoa, and confectioners' sugar. Whisk in the milk, eggs, and oil.

Coat a crepe pan or 8" nonstick skillet with cooking spray and heat over medium heat. Pour in 2 tablespoons of the batter, quickly tilting the pan in all directions to evenly spread the batter into a circle. Cook the crepe for 45 seconds, or until it easily comes loose from the pan. Flip the crepe over and cook the other side for 30 seconds. Place on a piece of waxed paper. Repeat with the remaining batter to make 12 crepes, layering the crepes between pieces of waxed paper. Set aside.

To make the filling: In a large bowl, with an electric mixer on medium speed, combine the ricotta, confectioners' sugar, vanilla extract, and liqueur until light and fluffy. Gently fold in the cherries.

Evenly divide the filling among the crepes. Fold each crepe in half, then in half again. Arrange on a serving plate. Sprinkle with the preserves.

Makes 12 crepes

Per serving: 214 calories, 7 g protein, 29 g carbohydrates, 8 g fat, 57 mg cholesterol, 0 g fiber, 55 mg sodium

COOKING TIP

A crepe pan works best for cooking crepes, but if you don't have one, a slope-sided skillet works fine.

Confetti Cannoli

16 ounces ricotta cheese

½ cup confectioners' sugar + additional for garnish

1 teaspoon vanilla extract

¼ teaspoon almond extract

½ cup candy-coated mini baking bits

8 prepared cannoli shells

You'll find a rainbow of color—and flavor—in these fun and festive cannoli. And the best part is, there's no baking involved. Just whip up the filling and pipe into the premade shells. It couldn't be easier!

In a large bowl, with an electric mixer on medium speed, beat the cheese, confectioners' sugar, vanilla extract, and almond extract until well-blended. Stir in the baking bits.

Just before serving, spoon the ricotta mixture into a pastry bag fitted with a large plain tip. Pipe the ricotta filling into the cannoli shells from both ends. Sprinkle with the additional confectioners' sugar.

Makes 8 cannoli

Per serving: 257 calories, 8 g protein, 23 g carbohydrates, 15 g fat, 29 mg cholesterol, 1 g fiber, 49 mg sodium

Chocolate Cannoli

16 square wonton skins

2 tablespoons butter, melted

1 teaspoon ground cinnamon

16 ounces ricotta cheese

½ cup confectioners' sugar

1 teaspoon vanilla extract

¼ cup semisweet chocolate chips, divided

1 teaspoon butter

For a change of pace, these cannoli use Asian wonton skins, but if you're in a hurry, you can substitute premade cannoli shells.

Preheat the oven to 400°F. Grease 2 baking sheets.

Brush both sides of a wonton skin with melted butter. Sprinkle with the cinnamon. Shape into a tube by curling opposite corners around a cannoli mold or whisk handle. Place, seam side down, on the prepared baking sheet. Repeat to make a total of 16 shells. Bake for 7 minutes, or until lightly browned at the edges and set. Remove from the oven and let stand for 3 minutes, or until the shells have cooled on the molds and are crisp. Gently slide them off.

In a large bowl, with an electric mixer on medium speed, beat the cheese, confectioners' sugar, and vanilla extract until well-blended. Stir in 2 tablespoons of the chocolate chips. Cover and refrigerate until ready to serve.

Just before serving, spoon the ricotta mixture into a pastry bag fitted with a large plain tip. Pipe the ricotta filling into the cannoli shells from both ends.

Place the remaining 2 tablespoons chocolate chips and the 1 teaspoon butter in a small microwaveable bowl. Microwave on high, stirring every 20 seconds, until the chocolate is almost melted. Stir until completely melted and smooth. Using a fork, drizzle over the cannoli.

Makes 16 cannoli

Per serving: 115 calories, 4 g protein, 10 g carbohydrates, 6 g fat, 20 mg cholesterol, 0 g fiber, 88 mg sodium

COOKING TIP

To shape the shells, you can use small (½" diameter) cannoli molds, available at baking supply shops and through mail-order catalogs.

Chocolate Chip Blintzes with Maple Drizzle

Filling

1⅔ cups cottage cheese

4 ounces cream cheese, softened

1 egg, beaten

¼ cup sugar

1 teaspoon vanilla extract

¼ cup mini semisweet chocolate chips

Blintzes

1 cup + 2 tablespoons milk

1 egg

1 tablespoon canola oil

1 teaspoon vanilla extract

1 cup unbleached all-purpose flour

1 teaspoon sugar

Pinch of salt

1 tablespoon butter, melted

1 tablespoon cinnamon sugar

¼ cup pure maple syrup, warmed, if desired

A blintz is a thin pancake stuffed with a cheesy filling and then baked. This version teams cream cheese and chocolate chips to create a very special confection.

To make the filling: Place the cottage cheese and cream cheese in a food processor or blender and process until smooth. Place in a medium bowl. Stir in the egg, sugar, and vanilla extract until well-blended. Stir in the chocolate chips. Refrigerate until ready to serve.

To make the blintzes: Rinse out the blender or food processor. Add the milk, egg, oil, and vanilla extract. Process to combine. Add the flour, sugar, and salt. Process until thoroughly combined.

Coat a medium nonstick skillet with cooking spray and heat over medium-high heat. Pour ¼ cup of the batter into the skillet, quickly tilting the pan in all directions to evenly spread the batter into a circle. Cook for 1 minute per side, or until lightly browned. Place on a plate and cover with a kitchen towel to keep warm. Repeat with the remaining batter to make a total of 8 blintzes, layering the blintzes between pieces of waxed paper.

Preheat the oven to 350°F. Grease a 13" x 9" baking dish.

Evenly divide the filling among the blintzes. Fold in all 4 sides to enclose the filling. Place the blintzes, seam side down, in the prepared baking dish. Brush the tops with melted butter, then sprinkle with cinnamon sugar. Bake for 25 minutes, or until the filling is hot. To serve, arrange 2 blintzes on each serving plate. Drizzle with the maple syrup.

Makes 8 blintzes

Per serving: 309 calories, 11 g protein, 34 g carbohydrates, 14 g fat, 84 mg cholesterol, 0 g fiber, 315 mg sodium

Blintz Soufflé

1 package (13 ounces) frozen apple, blueberry, or cherry blintzes (6 blintzes)

3 eggs

1 cup (8 ounces) sour cream

½ cup sugar

¼ cup orange juice

1 teaspoon vanilla extract

2 tablespoons packed brown sugar

Super-thin prepared blintzes form the crust for this unusual soufflé. The filling is a creamy combination with a bright, fresh orange flavor.

Preheat the oven to 350°F. Line the frozen blintzes in a 9" x 5" loaf pan.

In a medium bowl, whisk together the eggs, sour cream, sugar, orange juice, and vanilla extract until well-blended. Pour over the blintzes, then sprinkle with the brown sugar.

Bake for 1 hour, or until the filling is set. Let stand for 5 minutes before serving.

Makes 6 servings

Per serving: 304 calories, 7 g protein, 44 g carbohydrates, 11 g fat, 138 mg cholesterol, 1 g fiber, 69 mg sodium

Lace Cookies with Sorbet

¼ **cup butter**

⅓ **cup packed brown sugar**

¼ **cup light corn syrup**

½ **cup unbleached all-purpose flour**

¼ **cup finely chopped almonds**

⅛ **teaspoon salt**

Raspberry or other flavor sorbet

Fresh raspberries for garnish

These crispy cookies are actually shaped into delicate cups to hold sorbet or whatever strikes your fancy. Kids will enjoy being able to eat the "bowl."

Preheat the oven to 375°F. Grease 2 large baking sheets.

In a medium saucepan, combine the butter, brown sugar, and corn syrup. Bring to a boil over medium heat, stirring constantly, until the sugar is dissolved. Remove from the heat. Stir in the flour, almonds, and salt until well-blended. Drop 3 heaping teaspoonfuls, 3" apart, onto the prepared baking sheets (bake 3 per sheet).

Bake for 4 minutes, or until browned. Allow the cookies to cool on the baking sheets for 1 minute. Working quickly with a metal spatula, remove the cookies from the baking sheets and drape over the bottoms of upside-down custard cups. Cool completely. Repeat with the remaining batter to make a total of 18 cookies.

To serve, spoon sorbet into the cookie cups and garnish with the raspberries.

Makes 18 cookies

Per serving: 76 calories, 1 g protein, 10 g carbohydrates, 4 g fat, 7 mg cholesterol, 0 g fiber, 55 mg sodium

COOKING TIP

These cookies take practice, but they're well worth the effort. When baking, remember that the cookies can only be formed when they're hot, so the key is to work quickly. Work in batches, placing no more than 3 cookies on a baking sheet, so that you can quickly mold the baked cookies while the next batch is in the oven.

Profiteroles

Cream Puffs

1   cup water
½   cup butter
¼   teaspoon salt
1   cup unbleached all-
    purpose flour
4   eggs

Pastry Cream

1   tablespoon cornstarch
1   cup milk
1   whole egg
1   egg yolk
¼   cup sugar
    Pinch of salt
2   tablespoons butter
1   teaspoon vanilla extract
2   teaspoons liqueur, such
    as Grand Marnier or
    amaretto (optional)
    Confectioners' sugar

These are actually mini cream puffs, packed with a wonderfully rich pastry cream filling. The shape of profiteroles is whimsically irregular, so don't fret if they don't look "perfect."

To make the cream puffs: Preheat the oven to 400°F.

In a medium saucepan, bring the water, butter, and salt to a boil over high heat. Stir in the flour until smooth. Reduce the heat to low and cook, stirring constantly, for 30 seconds, or until the mixture forms a ball. Remove from the heat.

Beat in the eggs, one at a time, until blended and smooth. Drop by rounded teaspoons about 1½" apart onto ungreased baking sheets. Bake for 22 minutes, or until puffed and golden. Cool completely on a rack.

To make the pastry cream: In a medium bowl, whisk together the cornstarch and ¼ cup of the milk until the cornstarch is dissolved. Whisk in the whole egg and egg yolk. Set aside.

In a medium saucepan, combine the remaining ¾ cup milk, sugar, and salt. Bring to a boil over medium heat.

Slowly whisk about 1 cup of the milk mixture into the egg mixture. Whisk back into the saucepan and cook, whisking constantly, for 2 minutes, or until the mixture thickens. Remove from the heat. Whisk in the butter, vanilla extract, and liqueur, if using. Pour the pastry cream into a glass bowl and cover with plastic wrap against the surface. Refrigerate for 1 hour, or until cold.

Pierce the bottom of each puff with a knife. Spoon the chilled pastry cream into a plastic food storage bag and snip ¼" off one corner of the bag. Pipe the cream into each puff. Arrange on a serving plate and dust with confectioners' sugar.

Makes 56 profiteroles

Per serving: 42 calories, 1 g protein, 3 g carbohydrates, 3 g fat, 29 mg cholesterol, 0 g fiber, 47 mg sodium

Banana Split Cream Puffs

1   cup water

½   cup butter

¼   teaspoon salt

1   cup unbleached all-purpose flour

4   eggs

6   bananas, cut in half crosswise, then cut in half lengthwise

1   quart vanilla ice cream

2¼   cups hot fudge sauce, warmed

     Whipped cream for garnish (optional)

These cream puffs are served up sundae style, complete with bananas, hot fudge sauce, and the all-important whipped cream. You can vary the filling to suit your mood—try fresh strawberries with strawberry ice cream or peaches with peach ice cream.

Preheat the oven to 400°F. In a medium saucepan, bring the water, butter, and salt to a boil over high heat. Stir in the flour all at once until smooth. Reduce the heat to low and cook, stirring constantly, for 30 seconds, or until the mixture forms a ball. Remove from the heat.

Beat in the eggs, one at a time, until blended and smooth. Drop the dough by scant ¼ cupfuls about 3" apart onto ungreased baking sheets.

Bake for 35 to 40 minutes, or until puffed and golden. Cool completely on a rack.

Cut off the top third of each puff and remove the inner moist areas. Place the puffs on serving plates. Evenly divide the bananas and ice cream among the puffs. Drizzle with hot fudge sauce and replace the puff tops. Garnish with whipped cream, if using.

Makes 12 servings

Per serving: 479 calories, 8 g protein, 69 g carbohydrates, 20 g fat, 113 mg cholesterol, 3 g fiber, 386 mg sodium

Frozen Lemon Meringues

3   **egg whites, at room temperature**
¼   **teaspoon cream of tartar**
⅛   **teaspoon salt**
¾   **cup sugar**
½   **teaspoon vanilla extract**
2   **cups lemon sorbet**
    Fresh berries for garnish

With the aid of the freezer, serving this elegant dessert to company is nearly effortless. You can prepare the crisp yet cloudlike meringue shells ahead and freeze them (see tip).

Preheat the oven to 225°F. Line a large baking sheet with foil or parchment paper.

Place the egg whites in a large bowl. With an electric mixer on medium speed, beat until foamy. Add the cream of tartar and salt and beat until soft peaks form. Gradually beat in the sugar until the meringue is stiff and shiny. Beat in the vanilla extract.

Spoon the meringue into 4 large mounds evenly spaced on the prepared baking sheet. With the back of a spoon, form the meringue into 4" nests. Bake for 1 hour. Turn off the oven and allow the meringues to stand with the door closed for 1 hour. Remove from the oven and cool on a rack.

To serve, spoon ½ cup sorbet into each meringue shell and garnish with berries.

Makes 4 servings
Per serving: 275 calories, 3 g protein, 67 g carbohydrates, 0 g fat, 0 mg cholesterol, 1 g fiber, 134 mg sodium

---

COOKING TIP

To freeze, place the cooled meringue shells on a baking sheet in the freezer for 30 minutes, or until the meringues are solid. Place the shells in an air-tight container and freeze for up to 3 months. To use, thaw at room temperature for 30 minutes.

Mocha Meringue Kisses

2 tablespoons unsweetened cocoa powder

1 tablespoon unbleached all-purpose flour

¼ teaspoon instant espresso powder

2 large egg whites

⅛ teaspoon salt

½ cup sugar

The cocoa powder and espresso powder combine to give these divine little drops just a kiss of mocha. They look especially pretty on a dressed-up dessert buffet.

Preheat the oven to 225°F. Line 2 large baking sheets with foil or parchment paper.

In a small bowl, combine the cocoa powder, flour, and espresso powder. Set aside.

In a large bowl, with an electric mixer on medium speed, beat the egg whites and salt until foamy. With the mixer on high speed, gradually beat in the sugar until stiff peaks form and the mixture is glossy. Fold in the cocoa mixture just until blended.

Drop the meringue by rounded teaspoons onto the prepared baking sheets. Bake for 1 hour. Turn off the oven and allow the meringues to stand with the door closed for 1 hour. Cool on racks.

Makes 42 cookies

Per serving: 11 calories, 0 g protein, 3 g carbohydrates, 0 g fat, 0 mg cholesterol, 0 g fiber, 12 mg sodium

Cherry-Almond Turnovers

½ package (17¼ ounces) frozen puff pastry sheets (1 sheet)

1 package (16 ounces) frozen unsweetened pitted dark sweet cherries (about 1¾ cups)

¼ cup sugar

3 teaspoons cornstarch

1½ tablespoons brandy or water

4 tablespoons almond paste

1 tablespoon butter, melted

2 tablespoons sliced almonds

Flaky puff pastry encases a brandied cherry filling in this sweet treat. You can find almond paste in the baking aisle of most supermarkets.

Thaw the pastry sheet at room temperature for 30 minutes. Preheat the oven to 400°F.

In a medium saucepan over medium heat, combine the cherries (with any juice) and sugar. Cook, stirring, for 3 minutes, or until the sugar is dissolved and the cherries are heated through. In a cup, dissolve the cornstarch in the brandy or water. Gently stir into the cherry mixture and bring to a boil over medium-high heat. Boil for 2 minutes, or until the sauce is thickened. Remove from the heat. Place in a bowl, cover, and refrigerate until cool.

Unfold the pastry onto a lightly floured surface. Using a floured rolling pin, roll into a 12" square. Cut into 4 equal 6" squares and arrange on an ungreased baking sheet.

Crumble 1 tablespoon almond paste in the center of each square, leaving a 1" border. Evenly divide the cherry filling among the squares. Brush the edges of the squares with water, then fold each square into a triangle. Using a fork, decoratively seal the edges. Brush the tops with the melted butter and sprinkle with the almonds. Bake for 20 minutes, or until golden.

Makes 4 turnovers

Per serving: 298 calories, 4 g protein, 34 g carbohydrates, 14 g fat, 8 mg cholesterol, 2 g fiber, 63 mg sodium

Apple Strudel

2   medium Granny Smith or Golden Delicious apples, peeled, cored, and thinly sliced (about 3 cups)

2   tablespoons golden raisins

¼   cup packed brown sugar

½   teaspoon ground cinnamon

¼   teaspoon freshly ground nutmeg

⅓   cup plain dry bread crumbs

¼   cup granulated sugar

12   sheets (17" x 11") frozen phyllo dough, thawed

½   cup butter, melted

½   cup apricot all-fruit spread, warmed

1   tablespoon confectioners' sugar

The thawed frozen phyllo dough lets you avoid making fresh strudel dough, and it bakes up just as crispy and flaky. An unbaked strudel will freeze, tightly wrapped, for up to 3 months.

Preheat the oven to 400°F. Line a baking sheet with parchment paper.

In a large bowl, combine the apples, raisins, brown sugar, cinnamon, and nutmeg.

In a small bowl, combine the bread crumbs and granulated sugar.

Remove 12 sheets of thawed phyllo from the package and cover the remaining phyllo with a damp towel. Place 1 sheet on a work surface. Generously brush the phyllo with the melted butter. Sprinkle with 1 scant tablespoon of the crumb mixture. Repeat layering with 5 of the remaining phyllo sheets, topping the last sheet of phyllo with the butter only.

Spread the top sheet of phyllo with ¼ cup of the all-fruit spread to within 1" of the edges. Spoon half of the apple mixture over the fruit spread to within 1" of the edges. Fold 1" of each long edge of the phyllo over the apple mixture. Starting with the short edge, roll up as tightly as possible. Gently place the strudel, seam side down, on the prepared baking sheet. Repeat to make a second strudel. Place on the baking sheet. Brush both strudels with any remaining butter and sprinkle with any remaining crumbs. Using a sharp knife, make several slashes in the top of each strudel.

Bake for 15 minutes, or until crisp and golden brown. Sprinkle with the confectioners' sugar. Serve warm.

Makes 12 servings
Per serving: 232 calories, 2 g protein, 35 g carbohydrates, 10 g fat, 22 mg cholesterol, 1 g fiber, 207 mg sodium

Lemon-Cheese Strudel

12 ounces ricotta cheese

1 egg, beaten

¾ cup + 1 tablespoon granulated sugar

1 teaspoon vanilla extract

⅓ cup plain dry bread crumbs

12 sheets (17" x 11") frozen phyllo dough, thawed

½ cup butter, melted

1 cup prepared lemon curd

1 tablespoon confectioners' sugar

This pastry is a sunny lemon delight. You can find prepared lemon curd in the baking aisle of most supermarkets.

In a medium bowl, combine the cheese, egg, ½ cup of the granulated sugar, and vanilla extract just until blended. Set aside.

Preheat the oven to 375°F. Grease a baking sheet.

In a small bowl, combine the bread crumbs and ¼ cup of the remaining granulated sugar.

Remove 12 sheets of thawed phyllo from the package and cover the remaining phyllo with a damp towel. Place 1 sheet on a work surface. Generously brush the phyllo with the melted butter. Sprinkle with 2 scant teaspoons of the bread crumb mixture. Repeat layering with 5 of the remaining phyllo sheets, the melted butter, and the remaining bread crumb mixture.

Mound half of the cheese filling along one narrow end, leaving a 1" border on all sides. Spoon half of the lemon curd in dollops over the cheese filling. Fold 1" of each long edge of the phyllo over the filling. Starting with the short edge, roll up as tightly as possible. Gently place the strudel, seam side down, on the prepared baking sheet. Repeat to make a second strudel. Place on the baking sheet. Brush each strudel with any remaining butter and sprinkle with the remaining 1 tablespoon granulated sugar.

Bake for 25 minutes, or until crisp and golden. Cool on a rack for 15 minutes. Sprinkle with the confectioners' sugar.

Makes 12 servings

Per serving: 321 calories, 7 g protein, 33 g carbohydrates, 18 g fat, 100 mg cholesterol, 1 g fiber, 281 mg sodium

Index

Boldface references indicate photographs.

C